Academic Vocabulary for Middle School Students

Academic Vocabulary for Middle School Students

Research-Based Lists and Strategies for Key Content Areas

by

Jennifer Wells Greene, Ph.D.
Georgia Gwinnett College
Lawrenceville

and

Averil Coxhead, Ph.D.
Victoria University
Wellington, New Zealand

·P·A·U·L·H·
BROOKES
PUBLISHING C⁰ ®

Baltimore • London • Sydney

Paul H. Brookes Publishing Co.
Post Office Box 10624
Baltimore, Maryland 21285–0624

www.brookespublishing.com

Typeset by Scribe, Inc., Philadelphia, Pennsylvania.
Manufactured in the United States of America by
Sheridan Books, Chelsea, Michigan.

Library of Congress Cataloging-in-Publication Data

The Library of Congress has cataloged the print edition as follows:

Greene, Jennifer Wells.
    Academic vocabulary for middle school students : research-based lists and strategies for key content areas / Jennifer Wells Greene, Ph.D., Georgia Gwinnett College, Lawrenceville, Georgia, and Averil Coxhead, Ph.D., Victoria University, Wellington, New Zealand.
        pages   cm
    ISBN 978-1-59857-305-3 (paperback)—ISBN 1-589857-305-5—
ISBN 978-1-59857-583-5 (epub)—ISBN 1-59857-583-X (epub)
    1. Vocabulary—Study and teaching (Middle school)   I. Coxhead, Averil.   II. Title.

    LB1631.G736 2015
    428.10712—dc23   2014035220

British Library Cataloguing in Publication data are available from the British Library.

2019   2018   2017   2016   2015

10   9   8   7   6   5   4   3   2   1

Contents

About the Reproducible Materials

Purchasers of this book may download, print, and/or photocopy Appendix C for educational use. These materials are included with the print book and are also available at **http://www.brookespublishing.com/greene/materials** for both print and e-book buyers.

About the Authors

Jennifer Wells Greene, Ph.D., is an assistant professor in the School of Education at Georgia Gwinnett College in Lawrenceville, Georgia. Her research interests include specialized vocabulary in elementary and middle school education, as well as supporting grade-level teachers who want to incorporate word learning in their content-area classrooms. Dr. Greene is a literacy-teacher educator currently working with preservice teachers preparing for teaching certification.

Averil Coxhead, Ph.D., is a senior lecturer in applied linguistics in the School of Linguistics and Applied Language Studies at Victoria University in Wellington, New Zealand. Her research interests include specialized vocabulary in secondary and university-level education, the development and measurement of vocabulary size, the vocabulary load of written texts, and vocabulary in the trades. Dr. Coxhead teaches undergraduate and postgraduate applied linguistics and supervises Ph.D. research in vocabulary studies, English for academic purposes, and applied corpus linguistics.

Acknowledgments

This book is the product of years of research and development, and we are so appreciative of the guidance, support, and feedback we have received throughout the process. First, we wish to thank our colleagues and students who have helped shaped our thinking and writing over the years, specifically Joyce Many, Diane Belcher, Patricia Byrd, Gertrude Tinker-Sachs, and Xiaoxue Wang from Georgia State University, each of whom supervised the original research for this book. We would also like to thank Paul Nation and the reviewers for reading and commenting on the manuscript. Your thoughts helped us produce a much stronger book. Working with the team at Paul H. Brookes Publishing Co. has been a phenomenal experience. Together, we have produced a book that makes us proud. Finally, we wish to express our gratitude to the National Institute of Continuing Education and the University System of Georgia's Reading Consortium. This work could not have been completed without financial support from these institutions.

For Jane Greene and Beverley Coxhead,
inspiring teachers and wonderful mothers

Introduction

This is a book about the vocabulary needs of students in middle school and the development and use of a group of word lists to help these students and their teachers. When students are in the early elementary grades (kindergarten through third grade, ages 5–9 years), they are learning to read, and it is sufficient for them to know their grade-level words: if they master that much vocabulary, they can understand what they read. However, once they reach fourth grade (ages 9–10) and beyond, the curriculum changes; they are required to read independently in various content areas, and they begin to encounter more difficult words such as *approximate* and *fundamental*. Words such as these are part of a specialized vocabulary, academic vocabulary, that students encounter in their schoolwork but not in other aspects of their lives. Therefore, when students are at the stage of reading to learn, they often encounter too many unknown words, and comprehension suffers as a result. Teachers see this phenomenon play out every day in their classrooms, but with so much on their daily agenda they may not understand how to address the needs of these struggling students. The first step is to understand how many words these learners need to know for their studies.

HOW MANY WORDS DOES A MIDDLE SCHOOL STUDENT NEED TO KNOW?

Researchers have worked to understand the number of words students need to know in order to participate in different types of activities. They have learned that there are differences in the quantities and types of vocabulary needed for having a conversation or socializing with friends, for reading for pleasure, and for reading to learn. We will describe these differences in the following subsections.

How Many Words Do Middle School Students Need for Conversation?

Teachers of students who arrive at school knowing very little or no English at all are often surprised by how quickly their new students learn to communicate with friends in English. It has been demonstrated that a newcomer can find a way to communicate with friends and teachers rapidly, in as few as 6 months to 2 years (Cummins, 1979, 1980). This is because the same words are used over and over again in daily conversation, and for English learners, those words quickly become part of their second-language vocabulary. Roughly 50–100 words account for a great percentage of the total number of words in any text, spoken or written, so it is likely that words such as *the, and, I, that, you,* and *to* will frequently appear in the texts students read and in the language they use every day.

It is excellent news for all students (and their teachers) that, in English, these very few words do the majority of the work. *Webster's Third New International Dictionary of the English Language* (Gove, 1963) has 267,000 entries. Researchers culled through all of those words and reduced them to 58,000 base words, which is still a tremendous number of words to know (Goulden, Nation, & Read, 1990; Nation, 2013). It is very fortunate, then, that middle school students do not need to know 58,000 words: just those that help them communicate with family and friends, participate in school activities, and function in their daily lives.

High-frequency vocabulary provides students with an excellent foundational vocabulary. A student who has a good understanding of high-frequency vocabulary has the ability to participate in conversation and communicate just about any idea. English speakers need about 3,000–7,000 word families plus proper nouns to understand about 95%–98% of spoken conversation. Similarly, viewers of the movie *Shrek* need 4,000–7,000 word families to understand 96%–98% of the words in the script (Nation, 2006). These numbers demonstrate the differences between the total number of words in English and those needed to participate in daily activities. As will be discussed in the next section, these numbers begin to increase when the requirements of reading and understanding different kinds of written texts are considered.

How Many Words Do Middle School Students Need for Reading Comprehension?

Knowing enough words to have a conversation or understand a movie is very different from the word knowledge middle school students (Grades

6–8, ages 11–14) will need in order to read and understand grade-level texts. Years of reading research demonstrate that students who can read and understand 97%–98% of the words in a given text can read that text independently. Readers who recognize and understand 90%–97% of the words in a text can still learn from that text with instructional support in word meaning and key ideas. However, if a reader's word recognition and understanding drops below 90%, then that text is too difficult for good comprehension, even with instructional support (Gillett, Temple, & Crawford, 2004).

If middle school students do not need to know all of the words in English, how do teachers decide which words are most important for these students to know? Well, that depends on the student's purpose. To read newspapers and novels in English, students will need to know 8,000–9,000 word families plus proper nouns (Nation, 2006). This coverage seems to be quite stable. It is the same whether the text is *The Hunger Games* or *Pride and Prejudice* (Coxhead, 2012). These numbers change, however, when students are required to read content-area textbooks.

In a study of a series of New Zealand science textbooks written for students in Grades 9–12 (age ranges between 12 and 17 years), Coxhead, Stevens, and Tinkle (2010) found that 12- to 13-year-old (Grade 9) students needed to know more than 9,000 words to read a science textbook. Greene (2008) analyzed an eighth-grade science textbook for middle school students in the United States and found that students would need to know 7,000 words to recognize 95% of the words in the text.

These studies show that today's middle school students, who are expected to read and learn from their textbooks, need academic language skills beyond those required to have a conversation, watch a movie, or read a novel. Zwiers, O'Hara, and Pritchard (2014) described students learning to communicate using academic language as *academic English learners*. Recent immigrants certainly fall into this category, as do students from English-speaking homes who speak a variety or dialect of English that is incompatible with academic English. In addition, many students have grown up in English-speaking homes but for whatever reason still have difficulties with the rigors of academic English.

With the advent of the Common Core State Standards (CCSS) and their focus on in-depth learning from informational text, it becomes even more critical that teachers identify the academic language that middle school students need to know if they are to read and understand grade-level textbooks or to write at levels of expectation in their various content-area courses. Beyond this, the highest stakes are the students' academic careers and their futures as productive adults. We will examine the heightened demands of students' knowledge of academic language as they are reflected in the CCSS in the next section.

WHAT DO THE COMMON CORE STATE STANDARDS SAY ABOUT ACADEMIC LANGUAGE FOR MIDDLE SCHOOL STUDENTS?

The CCSS (National Governors Association Center for Best Practices & Council of Chief State School Officers [NGA Center for Best Practices & CCSSO], 2010) demonstrate three significant shifts in learning priorities for students in K–12 settings (Kapinus, Pimental, & Dean, 2012). The first shift is an increase in text complexity at each grade level, with an emphasis on nonfiction text over fictional text and the added requirement of understanding the academic language contained in nonfiction text. Currently, middle school students read about 85% fiction and 15% nonfiction text in their studies. Under the CCSS, these percentages change to 55% nonfiction text and 45% fictional text throughout middle school. Remember that nonfiction text is more difficult to read than fiction, so students will be required to read in a more challenging genre with increased grade-level complexity and to use careful, close reading strategies while doing so.

In addition, the CCSS emphasize that students should be able to recognize and use academic language throughout their coursework. Teachers may recall the hours they spent preparing for college-entrance exams. Many teachers spent a lot of time memorizing the meanings of really obscure words, and more than likely, they have not encountered those words again since they took those exams. Under the CCSS, those days are gone; the new priority for students is to read and understand the frequently occurring types of academic language (i.e., academic vocabulary) they encounter when working with expository text.

The second shift in learning priorities under the CCSS focuses on what students should take away from their reading. As an example, teachers of reading have been focused on their students' abilities to make inferences. With this goal in mind, they have asked students to respond to what they read by making connections between what is in the text and their personal experiences and ideas. Although these can be meaningful activities, they also allow students to move away from the text in their responses, rather than paying close attention to the information contained in the text. The CCSS require that students take away something very different from their reading: evidence. They require that students' responses to text be grounded in evidence taken from the text(s) they have read. Furthermore, students are required to use academic language throughout their oral and/or written responses (see NGA Center for Best Practices & CCSSO [ELA/Literacy Standards, Appendix A], 2010, pp. 2–4 for an in-depth discussion of these ideas).

The final shift relates to increasing student knowledge. The CCSS has literacy standards for science, social studies, mathematics, and other technical subjects, in addition to English language arts, and students are required to synthesize their understandings both within and across multiple informational texts as well as across content areas. In addition, there is a new focus on regular research projects in all content areas. To meet the standards, middle school students will need to demonstrate what they have learned from careful reading of nonfiction text by directly citing evidence in those texts to support whatever claims or inferences they are making—and they will be required to use academic language to do so.

The CCSS are rigorous, are evidence-based, and require higher-order thinking skills. The need for domain-specific academic vocabulary is demonstrated throughout the Grade 6–8 standards. Within the English language arts standards, vocabulary acquisition is a unique strand throughout the grade levels. Appendix A of the English language arts strand contains a specific discussion regarding academic vocabulary (see NGA Center for Best Practices & CCSSO [ELA/Literacy Standards, Appendix A], 2010, pp. 32–35). In addition, domain-specific academic vocabulary knowledge is also required in reading, writing, speaking, and listening standards for history/social studies, science, and technical subjects. Table I.1 contains the standards that address academic vocabulary knowledge specifically; however, it should be noted that the need for academic vocabulary is embedded throughout the standards. For example, in the writing standards for Grade 6 students, the first standard is to "Introduce claim(s) and organize the reasons and evidence clearly" (NGA Center for Best Practices & CCSSO [Writing Standards], 2010, p. 42). A further example of the need for academic vocabulary is found in the speaking and listening standards (Grades 6–8). The first standard requires that students "Come to discussions prepared, having read or studied required material; explicitly draw on that preparation by referring to evidence on the topic, text, or issue to probe and reflect on ideas under discussion" (NGA Center for Best Practices & CCSSO [Speaking and Listening Standards], 2010, p. 49). As discussed earlier, the CCSS require students to use academic language while reading and responding to text. It would be difficult, if not impossible, for a student to meet this standard (and others throughout the document) without a good control of academic vocabulary appropriate for the subject area and grade level.

Common Core State Standards and English Language Learners

Guidance about using the CCSS with English language learners (ELLs) does not focus on vocabulary knowledge specifically, except in its discussion of the application of mathematical standards. That said, the CCSS focus on the need for ELLs to become "proficient and literate in English," as well as for providing instruction that "develops foundational skills in English and enables ELLs to participate fully in grade-level coursework" (NGA Center for Best Practices & CCSSO [Application of Common Core State Standard for English Language Learners], 2010, p. 2). Vocabulary knowledge, specifically the knowledge of the particular words ELLs will

Table I.1.   Alignment of the Common Core State Standards and academic vocabulary (Grades 6–8)

Strands	Common Core State Standards (CCSS) and academic vocabulary: Grades 6, 7, and 8
English language arts	
Reading informational texts	Determine the meanings of words and phrases as they are used in a text, including figurative, connotative, and technical meanings (CCSS.ELA-Literacy.RI.6.4; CCSS.ELA-Literacy.RI.7.4; CCSS.ELA-Literacy.RI.8.4). By the end of the year, read and comprehend literary nonfiction in the Grades 6–8 complexity band, with scaffolding as needed at the high end of the range (CCSS.ELA-Literacy.RI.6.10; CCSS.ELA-Literacy.RI.7.10; CCSS.ELA-Literacy.RI.8.10).
Writing	Use words, phrases, and clauses to create cohesion and clarify the relationships among claim(s), reasons, and evidence (CCSS.ELA-Literacy.W.6.1c; CCSS.ELA-Literacy.W.7.1c; CCSS.ELA-Literacy.W.8.1c). Establish and maintain a formal style (CCSS.ELA-Literacy.W.6.1d; CCSS.ELA-Literacy.W.7.1d; CCSS.ELA-Literacy.W.8.1d). Use precise language and domain-specific vocabulary to inform about or explain the topic (CCSS.ELA-Literacy.W.6.2d; CCSS.ELA-Literacy.W.7.2d; CCSS.ELA-Literacy.W.8.2d).
Speaking and listening	Come to discussions prepared, having read or studied required material; explicitly draw on that preparation by referring to evidence on the topic, text, or issue to probe and reflect on ideas under discussion (CCSS.ELA-Literacy.SL.6.1a; CCSS.ELA-Literacy.SL.7.1a; CCSS.ELA-Literacy.SL.8.1a). Pose and respond to specific questions with elaboration and detail by making comments that contribute to the topic, text, or issue under discussion (CCSS.ELA-Literacy.SL.6.1c; CCSS.ELA-Literacy.SL.7.1c; CCSS.ELA-Literacy.SL.8.1c).
Language	Use common, grade-appropriate Greek or Latin affixes and roots as clues to the meaning of a word (CCSS.ELA-Literacy.Literacy.L.6.4b; CCSS.ELA-Literacy.Literacy.L.7.4b; CCSS.ELA-Literacy.Literacy.L.8.4b). Acquire and use accurately grade-appropriate general academic and domain-specific words and phrases; gather vocabulary knowledge when considering a word or phrase important to comprehension (CCSS.ELA-Literacy.L.6.6; CCSS.ELA-Literacy.L.7.6; CCSS.ELA-Literacy.L.8.6).
Literacy in history/social studies, science, and technical subjects	
History/social studies	Determine the meaning of words and phrases as they are used in a text, including vocabulary specific to domains related to history/social studies (CCSS.ELA-Literacy.RH.6-8.10). By the end of Grade 8, read and comprehend history/social studies texts in the Grades 6–8 text complexity band independently and proficiently (CCSS.ELA-Literacy.RH.6-8.10).
Science and technical subjects	Determine the meaning of symbols, key terms, and other domain-specific words and phrases as they are used in a specific scientific or technical context relevant to Grades 6–8 texts and topics (CCSS.ELA-Literacy.RST.6-8.4). By the end of Grade 8, read and comprehend science/technical texts in the Grades 6–8 text complexity band independently and proficiently (CCSS.ELA-Literacy.RST.6-8.10).

Strands	Common Core State Standards (CCSS) and academic vocabulary: Grades 6, 7, and 8
Writing	Use precise language and domain-specific vocabulary to inform about or explain the topic (CCSS.ELA-Literacy.WHST.6-8.2d). Establish and maintain a formal style and objective tone (CCSS.ELA-Literacy.WHST.6-8.2f).

Source: Common Core State Standards © Copyright 2010 National Governors Association Center for Best Practices and Council of Chief State School Officers. All rights reserved.

encounter within their classroom discussions and textbook readings, is critical in meeting this requirement.

Common Core State Standards and Students with Disabilities

Vocabulary knowledge is not specifically mentioned in discussion of the CCSS and students with disabilities; however, it is clear that students with disabilities are expected to meet the same standards as those in general education classrooms with appropriate support and accommodations (NGA Center for Best Practices & CCSSO [Application to Students with Disabilities], 2010). For these students, too, knowledge of the academic vocabulary contained in their textbooks is vital for meeting those standards.

WHO IS THE AUDIENCE FOR THIS BOOK?

This book is written for teachers of middle school students, as well as for other professionals who work with students at this level. University-level faculty involved in preparing new teachers for the rigors of instruction under the CCSS will find the ideas in this book helpful as well.

This book has three distinct purposes. Our first purpose is to share the Middle School Vocabulary Lists with teachers, materials designers, and other professionals. Our second purpose is to help shape the reader's understanding of the different kinds of vocabulary (with a focus on academic vocabulary) that is found in content-area textbooks written for middle school students. Finally, we will share some ideas for prioritizing and focusing on these words in the classroom.

SUMMARY

Throughout the introduction, we have discussed the number of words middle school students need to know to participate in activities ranging from conversation to reading textbooks, realizing that the words in textbooks contain a different kind of vocabulary (academic vocabulary) that students do not encounter in other contexts. We have also described the shift in priorities for student learning set forth in the CCSS and the important role that academic vocabulary plays in these standards. In Chapter 1 we will discuss in detail the different kinds of vocabulary that can be found in middle school content-area textbooks and describe how a corpus-based methodology can be used to identify the academic vocabulary contained in these books. We will delve into the Middle School Vocabulary Lists throughout Chapter 2 and see how the words on these lists are integrated into middle school textbooks. We will demonstrate how to set instructional priorities for incorporating the words on these lists into classroom instruction in Chapter 3. Chapter 4 presents 14 vocabulary learning activities teachers can use when focusing on the words in the Middle School Vocabulary Lists. These lists can be found in Appendix A, and the methodology used to create the Middle School Vocabulary Lists are in Appendix B. In Chapter 5 we tackle the big idea, What Does It Mean to Know a Word?, and provide tools to determine how many words your students know now, using the Vocabulary Size Test (Coxhead, Nation, & Sim, 2014), which can be found in Appendix C.

Key Concepts and Ideas About Vocabulary

1

ANTICIPATION ACTIVITY

1. Note down 20 words you commonly teach in class and roughly categorize them into words you think your students already know and words you think they should know. Then rearrange them from the ones you think occur more often in English to the ones you think occur least often. Finally, categorize them into words that are closely related to the subject you teach and words that are not. Have these ranking activities with the 20 words influenced the way you think about whether your students should know these words? If so, why? If not, why not?

2. How would you define *academic vocabulary* for middle school students? Note down your definition and see how it relates to the discussion of academic vocabulary in this chapter.

3. What word lists do you know about and use in your teaching? What might be the advantages and disadvantages of using word lists with your students?

In this chapter we describe a frequency-based methodology for categorizing words in texts. We define *academic vocabulary* by comparing and contrasting it with high-frequency, technical, and low-frequency words, and we discuss some ideas related to the classification of proper nouns. From there we move into a discussion of the development of several well-known word lists created since the 1990s. Finally, we introduce the Middle School Vocabulary Lists found in Appendix A of this book (Greene, 2008), with a brief description of how they were developed.

HOW CAN WORDS IN TEXTS BE CATEGORIZED?

Categorizing words can be a very tricky process. Some words occur in all kinds of texts and everyday language. These are high-frequency words, which include words such as *go, do, and,* and *I.* A well-known categorization of vocabulary (Beck, McKeown, & Kucan, 2002) would categorize these words as *Tier 1 words,* or basic words. Other words clearly belong to a particular area or subject and tend not to occur anywhere else very often at all. An example of this kind of word in science class is *photosynthesis.* Such words can be called *technical words.* Beck et al. (2002) would label these words as *Tier 3 words,* which would be low-frequency words, or, like *photosynthesis,* those used in specific domains. This tiered categorization of words is somewhat similar to the frequency-based methodology corpus that researchers use to place words into four distinct categories: high-frequency vocabulary, specialized vocabulary that includes academic and technical vocabulary, and, finally, mid- and low-frequency vocabulary.

Some words can be categorized in different ways. Think about words like *Parkinson.* It can be an everyday family name, but it can also be the name of a medical condition. Is it an everyday word or is it a technical word? What about *accurate*? In everyday terms, it seems like a common word, but in physics it has a very particular meaning. Is *accurate* an everyday word or is it a technical word? The answer very much depends on the context and the needs of learners. Vocabulary researchers and teachers are both concerned with making sure that learners focus on the words that learners need for their studies, and yet words do not neatly fall into groups. In the next sections we will describe the specialized vocabulary (academic and technical vocabulary) that can be found in academic texts.

WHAT IS ACADEMIC VOCABULARY?

Words that exist frequently in academic texts, but not so frequently in other kinds of texts (e.g., novels), can be referred to as *academic vocabulary.* These words share some other interesting characteristics. First, they are often supportive to a topic, but not central to a topic. Consider the word *alternative,* which suggests an option or a choice. When this word is used, the writer or speaker is usually talking about a bigger idea, and this word helps support that big idea. Another characteristic of academic words is that they often come from Greek or Latin roots (e.g., *port* [to carry] in the words *transport* and *export*). Finally, academic words are not high-frequency words (Coxhead, 2000). Beck et al. (2002) would likely have considered academic vocabulary to be a part of a Tier 2 list. That being said, Beck et al. left decisions about placing a specific word in a specific tier to the teacher. We believe that frequency-based evidence can be a tremendous help in making this determination.

So, one definition for academic vocabulary might be that it is the vocabulary needed for school or university study. Teachers would expect this vocabulary to occur in texts that students read and would expect students to use these words in their writing and speaking for academic purposes. In addition, as students get older and start to specialize in particular fields of study, such as molecular biology or psycholinguistics, they need to learn specialized vocabulary, which contains both academic words and the technical terms related to their content areas. Now we will look at how the academic vocabulary for middle school students, for example, is different from technical vocabulary.

WHAT IS TECHNICAL VOCABULARY?

The second type of specialized vocabulary is *technical vocabulary*. Whereas academic words are common across a range of different texts (e.g., science, social studies, mathematics), technical words are frequent within a specific subject. Referring back to the idea of vocabulary tiers (Beck et al., 2002), these words would be classified as Tier 3 words because they are used in specific domains. Technical vocabulary is easy to recognize in a textbook, because the words are often bolded or italicized, or they are included in charts and diagrams.

Technical words are those important to know within a specific content area (e.g., *molecule* in science; *quadratic* in mathematics) but are not as important to know (in terms of frequency) outside that content area (Nation, 2013, p. 19). An interesting point about technical vocabulary, and one that makes research in this area sometimes difficult, is that some everyday words have a technical meaning when they are used in specific contexts. For example, *solution* in the sciences carries a very particular meaning that is different from *solution* when it is used in mathematics, yet both meanings of the word are used in everyday language. Something that is *significant* in statistics is quite different in meaning from a *significant* birthday in everyday use.

For this reason, it is important to identify the technical vocabulary within each content area. This makes it easier for students and teachers to isolate the specific meaning of that word as it is used in that area. The Middle School Vocabulary Lists in Appendix A contain many of the technical words students encounter within each of the five different content areas.

To demonstrate how academic and technical words play out in academic text, we include here a few paragraphs from a seventh-grade science textbook. The bolded words come from the Middle School Science Vocabulary List, and of those, words that are considered technical terms are also underlined.

> Every living thing is composed of one or more **cells**. A **cell** is a **membrane**-covered **structure** that contains all of the materials necessary for life. The **membrane** that surrounds a **cell** separates the contents of the **cell** from the **cell's environment**.
>
> Many **organisms**, such as those in Figure 1, are made up of only one **cell**. Other **organisms**, such as the monkeys and trees in Figure 2, are made up of trillions of **cells**. Most **cells** are too small to be seen with the naked eye.
>
> In an **organism** with many **cells**, **cells** perform specialized **functions**. For example, your **nerve cells** are specialized to **transport** signals, and your **muscle cells** are specialized for movement. (*Holt Science & Technology: Life Science*, 2004, p. 36)

A quick analysis shows that 20% of the words in these paragraphs are Middle School Science Vocabulary List words (each occurrence is bolded). Some of these are purely academic in nature (e.g., *environment*, *functions*, *structure*, *transport*) and others, such as *cell*, *membrane*, and *organism*, are technical terms (each occurrence is bolded and underlined). Note that *cell* is defined in the text immediately after it is introduced (i.e., "A cell is a membrane-covered structure that contains all of the materials necessary for life"). Providing definitions after the first mention of a technical word is very common in academic texts. However, notice that many Middle School Science Vocabulary List words are not defined in any way; yet, students would need to know their meanings if they wanted to read and understand these paragraphs. As an example, one of the Middle School Science Vocabulary List words (*structure*) that is not defined in this passage is used as part of the definition of the technical word *cell*.

WHAT IS HIGH-FREQUENCY VOCABULARY?

High-frequency vocabulary consists of the words people use frequently, either in speaking or in writing. The introduction to this book discussed the need for knowledge of the first couple thousand words to communicate in English every day and as a basis for reading comprehension of different texts. These high-frequency words really are the base layer of language that all learners need. Finding out exactly what these high-frequency word families are is not as easy as it may seem. Researchers have to consider many factors in order to determine which are the most frequent words in English; for example, what sources should be used to decide on those words? Would they be spoken or written texts? In what contexts? Who would be the speakers and the writers of those texts used in the list making? One example of a word list of the first 2,000 words is by Nation (2006), who used the British National Corpus. Another example is the Corpus of Contemporary American English lists by Mark Davies (2012) at Brigham Young University.

The General Service List (GSL; West, 1953) is a well-known list of high-frequency vocabulary created to provide people with a relatively short list of words that would allow them to communicate just about any idea. The resulting list contains about 2,000 word families. These words are simple words; for example, although many words exist to describe various shades of the color blue (e.g., *aqua, turquoise, azure, teal*), for the purposes of West's list, only the word *blue* was included. Note that the word *whistle* is also on this list. Even though that word is not used very often, there just is no other word in English that means the same thing as *whistle* (Nation, 1990). The GSL was created in the 1950s, and even though it is now quite old and does not contain words such as *computer* and *Internet*, it still provides consistent results when it is used to analyze the high-frequency words in most texts.

Many of the words on the GSL would correspond to Beck et al.'s (2002) Tier 1 words. In addition, GSL words can be found on sight-word lists (e.g., the Dolch [1948] and Fry [2006] lists) for students in the early stages of learning to read. These words are crucial for students to recognize and understand because they cover about 80% of written text across genres (Nation & Hwang, 1995). They appear in picture books, books for young readers and adolescents, novels, newspapers, and magazines, as well as textbooks written for middle school students (Greene, 2008), high school students, and students working toward university-level study (Coxhead, 2000).

The following are the top 10 words on the GSL (West, 1953):

> the (article)
> be (copular verb)
> of (preposition)
> and (conjunction)
> a (article)
> to (preposition)
> in (preposition)
> he (pronoun)
> have (copular verb)
> it (pronoun)

If someone asked you what these words meant, how would you answer that question? These examples reveal an interesting characteristic of some of the most frequently used words on the GSL. They are function words, carrying very little meaning (Nation, 2013); their greater purpose is to contribute to the grammar of a sentence. As an example, the most frequently used word in spoken and written English, *the*, has a definition that includes 18 different usage patterns and runs more than half a page in length in the *Collins COBUILD Advanced Learners Dictionary* (Sinclair, 2003). The remaining words on the GSL consist of content words (e.g., *tree, child, run*) that carry a great deal of meaning, thus making them easier to teach and learn.

To demonstrate how powerful this list really is, we will look at a paragraph from Lois Lowry's (1993) award-winning adolescent novel, *The Giver*. The words in this paragraph are coded to demonstrate where they fall on the GSL. Bolded words occur in the first 1,000 word families, and underlined words occur in the second 1,000 families. The remaining words are not part of the GSL.

> **It was almost December and** Jonas **was beginning to be** <u>frightened</u>. **No. Wrong word,** Jonas **thought.** <u>Frightened</u> **meant that deep,** sickening **feeling of something** <u>terrible</u> **about to happen.** <u>Frightened</u> **was the way he had felt a year ago when an** unidentified **aircraft had** overflown **the** community **twice. He had seen it both times.** Squinting **toward the sky, he had seen the** sleek jet, **almost a** blur **at its high speed, go past, and a second later he heard the** blast **of sound that followed. Then one more time, a moment later, from the** <u>opposite</u> **direction, the same** <u>plane</u>.
>
> **At first, he had only been** fascinated. **He had never seen** aircraft **so close, for it was against the rules for** pilots **to fly over the** community. **Occasionally, when supplies were** <u>delivered</u> **by** cargo <u>planes</u> **to the landing field across the river, the children rode bicycles to the** riverbank **and watched,** intrigued, **the** <u>unloading</u> **and then the** takeoff **directed to the west, always away from the** community. (p. 1)

There are 109 distinct words in these paragraphs, and of these, 92 (84%) are included on the GSL. This analysis provides an excellent demonstration of the coverage of this list, and it becomes clear how important the words on this list are to know.

The Giver is from a genre of literature referred to as fantasy fiction, so next we will look at another example from a different genre: nonfiction expository text written for eighth-grade students. The following paragraphs are taken from the first chapter of Prentice Hall's *Science Explorer: Physical Science* (Padilla et al., 2005). As in the text from *The Giver* quoted earlier, bolded words are from the first 1,000 word families on the GSL, underlined words are from the second 1,000 word families, and the remaining words are not on either list.

> **You have** <u>probably</u> **heard the word matter many times. Think about how often you hear the** phrases, **"As a matter of fact, . . ." or "**<u>Hey</u>, **what's the matter?" In science, this word has a** specific **meaning. Matter is anything that has mass and takes up space. All the "**<u>stuff</u>**" around you is matter, and you are matter too. Air,** plastic, **metal, wood, glass, paper, and** <u>cloth</u>— **all of these are matter.**
>
> **Even though air and** plastic **are both matter, no one has to tell you they are different materials. Matter can be hard or soft, rough or** <u>smooth</u>, **hot or cold,** <u>liquid</u>, <u>solid</u>, **or gas. Some materials catch fire easily, but others do not burn.** Chemistry **is the study of the properties of matter and how matter changes.** (pp. 34–35)

These two paragraphs contain 128 distinct words, and a whopping 96% are part of the GSL! Clearly, the ability to recognize and understand the words on the GSL provides a student a leg up in reading comprehension.

WHAT IS MID-FREQUENCY VOCABULARY?

New research is underway to define *mid-frequency vocabulary* (Schmitt & Schmitt, 2012). If groups of words are conceptualized into bands, the first band would be high-frequency words (2,000–3,000 words) and the next bands (3,000 to under 9,000) would be considered mid-frequency words. This idea of mid-frequency vocabulary is important, because it helps to bridge the gap between the number of words students need to communicate basic ideas (high-frequency vocabulary) and the number of words students need to independently participate in grade-level coursework. This work is still in its infancy, and researchers are debating where the line should be drawn between high-frequency and mid-frequency vocabulary (Nation, 2013); however, for ELLs especially, mid-frequency vocabulary should be an important learning goal.

WHAT IS LOW-FREQUENCY VOCABULARY?

Some words just are not used very often, regardless of the subject being discussed. We classify those words as *low-frequency vocabulary*. Beck et al. (2002) categorized this vocabulary (in addition to technical words) as Tier 3 vocabulary. In the previous section, we described vocabulary bands. Low-frequency vocabulary exists in the bands beyond 9,000 words (Schmitt & Schmitt, 2012). Compound words fall into this category. So do foreign words, abbreviations, and acronyms. Are you familiar with the word *gobbet*? It refers to a chunk of raw meat and is an excellent example of a low-frequency word.

There is a tricky thing about low-frequency vocabulary, though. Nation puts it this way: "One person's technical vocabulary is another person's low-frequency vocabulary" (2013, p. 29). If you teach fifth-grade science, you have probably taught a unit about the solar system and the phases of the moon. For you, the word *gibbous* would be a technical term (and maybe even a high-frequency term). However, we suspect that there are a tremendous number of people who have not read or used the word *gibbous* since their days in fifth grade, which would make *gibbous* part of their low-frequency vocabulary.

HOW CAN PROPER NOUNS BE CATEGORIZED?

Proper nouns, such as *Parkinson* mentioned earlier in this chapter, can be tricky for learners. Proper nouns can be viewed in two ways. One way is to say that these words are a kind of high-frequency vocabulary, in that they are a normal part of the text and they do not pose much of a learning burden. In *The Hunger Games* novels, for example, once readers know who Katniss is, they should have no more trouble with that word as they read through the novels. Another way of thinking about proper nouns is to treat them as technical words that learners need to know in order to understand written text. An interesting point about proper nouns is that they vary in number and type in subject areas. In medicine, place and people names are frequently used as names for diseases and conditions (e.g., *Parkinson's disease, Lou Gehrig's disease*). In history, place and people names may also occur, but they can also represent events (e.g., *Boer Wars, Gettysburg Address*). Also, proper nouns often carry meaning beyond being the name of a person or a place. Consider the proper nouns *Venice* and *Katrina*. Someone who is familiar with Venice may conjure an image of an old European city with canals instead of streets. Katrina is a woman's name, but it is also the name of a powerful hurricane that flooded the city of New Orleans.

These ideas demonstrate that teachers cannot assume that students will easily read and understand the meanings of proper nouns, because these words can carry a more difficult learning burden than they might expect (Erten & Razi, 2009; Kobeleva, 2008). For these reasons, teachers need to make instructional decisions about the proper nouns middle school students encounter, considering how much they need to know about them in order to understand their meanings in academic contexts.

RESEARCH ON WORD LISTS

Well-known vocabulary researcher and creator of the Compleat Lexical Tutor web site (http://www.lextutor.ca) Tom Cobb states, "Learners like word lists, so let's give them good ones" (n.d.). To do that, it is important to know the purpose of the learners and what they already know. Many such word lists have been developed to help teachers prioritize their vocabulary instruction, which in turn helps students comprehend the texts that will relay content-area knowledge. Many teachers are familiar with existing word lists such as "A List of Essential Words by Grade Level" (Marzano, Kendall, & Paynter, 2005), the Academic Vocabulary Word Lists (Marzano, 2002, 2004), Biemiller's (2010) *Words Worth Teaching*, and Coxhead's (2000) Academic Word List (AWL). These word lists are all part of a wealth of research on vocabulary since the 1990s, and they all take different approaches to the question of which words learners and teachers should spend their invaluable classroom time studying. Table 1.1 highlights these lists and the methodologies used to compile them, and we will describe them more fully in the remainder of this section.

"A List of Essential Words by Grade Level" (Marzano et al., 2005) was created with the goal of identifying the words that students would encounter when reading grade-level textbooks and standardized tests. The process for creating this list was extensive. The researchers began with the *Basic Elementary Reading Vocabulary* list (Harris & Jacobson, 1972). Due to the age of that list, a team of 60 teachers reviewed it and added words they thought were important or deleted words deemed

Table 1.1. Methodologies and features of commonly used word lists

Title	Methodology	Features
"A List of Essential Words by Grade Level" (Marzano, Kendall, & Paynter, 2005)	• List compiled from two earlier word lists • Expert opinion determined a word's inclusion on the list	• 6,768 words sorted by grade levels K–6
Academic Vocabulary Word Lists (Marzano, 2002, 2004)	• List compiled from standards documents • Focus on identifying instructional concepts contained in standards documents • Expert opinion determined an instructional concept's inclusion on the list	• 7,923 instructional concepts sorted into 13 content areas and four instructional levels
Words Worth Teaching (Biemiller, 2010)	• List derived from the Living Word Vocabulary (Dale & O'Rourke, 1981) • Word meaning(s) considered in development of this list	• 11,000 words including multiple meanings Words and their meanings are sorted into the grade levels in which a student should know secondary meanings
"A New Academic Word List" (Coxhead, 2000)	• List derived from 3.5-million-word corpus of written university-level text across multiple disciplines • Words included are not part of established high-frequency vocabulary	• 570 word families customized for students preparing for university-level study; sorted by frequency

unimportant. This reviewed list of words was then merged with another list (Becker, Dixon, & Anderson-Inman, 1980), which resulted in a combined list of more than 30,000 words. From there, the researchers omitted abbreviations, inflected forms, alternate forms, most proper names, formulas, foreign words, some forms of numbers, and feminine forms of nouns. The resulting list contained 6,768 words, which were then sorted into grade-level lists for students in Grades K–6.

The Academic Vocabulary Word Lists (Marzano, 2002, 2004) were developed to determine the essential instructional concepts described in standards documents for K–12 education in the United States. Rather than using textbooks or existing word lists, Marzano began with standards documents developed for 13 content areas. He used linguistic analysis to determine the primary instructional concepts contained in those standards. Those identified concepts were then grouped into categories. Finally, teams of experienced in-field educators reviewed the lists, and majority agreement determined which concepts were truly essential for students to know. The resulting list contains 7,923 instructional concepts, which are organized into 11 content areas and four instructional levels.

Biemiller's (2010) *Words Worth Teaching* was developed with a focus on meaning rather than frequency. To create his list, Biemiller began with *The Living Word Vocabulary* (Dale & O'Rourke, 1981), which provides word meanings that students could be expected to know at a particular grade level. With the understanding that words often share more than one meaning, this list shows at which grade level a secondary word meaning should be known. *The Living Word Vocabulary* is an older list, so Biemiller retested the word meanings to make sure that their placement was appropriate for students in primary and upper-elementary grades. The resulting list contains more than 11,000 word-meaning entries, including multiword units (e.g., *ways and means, you yourself*), proper nouns (e.g., *Gospels, Social Security*), compound words (e.g., *waterfowl, wristband*), hyphenated words (e.g., *court-martial, self-conscious*), phrasal verbs (e.g., *due to, turn out*), and acronyms (e.g., *G.I.*), and the words are coded to indicate the appropriate instructional level for the elementary grades.

Coxhead (2000) wanted to identify the academic words that occur frequently in university-level academic writing and developed a 3.5-million-word corpus of written texts students would encounter in the disciplines of arts, commerce, law, and science. The AWL contains the most frequently occurring word families within that corpus outside of the GSL. For students working toward university-level study, the AWL is a useful list because it is relatively short (570 word families) and represents about 10% of the text contained in Coxhead's Academic Corpus (for a detailed description of the development of the AWL, see Appendix B, pp. 145–146).

IDENTIFYING ACADEMIC VOCABULARY IN MIDDLE SCHOOL TEXTS

To improve middle school students' chances of academic success, researchers need to identify a list of words that occur most frequently in middle school textbooks but that are not considered high-frequency vocabulary. Greene (2008) followed Coxhead's (2000) AWL methodology to identify these words and collected 109 content-area textbooks used by middle school students. The resulting corpus contained more than 18 million words, and from that corpus come the Middle School Vocabulary Lists in Appendix A. These lists are broken down into five content areas—English Grammar and Writing, Health, Mathematics, Science, and Social Studies/History—and they are customized for middle school students' specific reading needs. The Middle School Vocabulary Lists cover a greater percentage of text written for middle school students than any of the other lists described above, which makes these lists far more powerful for middle school students to use.

SUMMARY

This chapter looked at the different kinds of vocabulary that middle school students need to read both fiction and nonfiction texts and explored the reasons why vocabulary lists are important for students and teachers. It also discussed some of the well-known vocabulary lists used today and briefly described the Middle School Vocabulary Lists that appear in this book. These lists are provided in Appendix A and will be discussed in depth in Chapter 2.

DISCUSSION QUESTIONS

1. Find a sample of text you regularly use in class that is roughly the same size as the samples of texts in this chapter. Read through the text and underline words you think will be in the first thousand words of English. Then type the text into the VocabProfiler on the Compleat Lexical Tutor web site (http://www.lextutor.ca) and check your predictions against the results from the computer analysis. What percentage of your text is from the first thousand and the second thousand words of English? What influence does this information have on the way you think about the vocabulary in that text for your students?

2. Look at the samples of texts in this chapter. Read through them again. Compare their vocabulary. What surprises or interests you in this analysis?

3. What effect might proper nouns have in your subject area? Which ones do you tend to teach or not teach? How do you check that your students know how to recognize proper nouns in texts?

2

The Middle School Vocabulary Lists in Context

ANTICIPATION ACTIVITY

1. What content area do you teach? Think about the academic words, those that are more supportive in nature across content areas (e.g., *perceive, respond*), and technical words, those that are important to know in a specific content area (e.g., *pronoun* in English grammar and writing, *atom* in science) you encounter when you are teaching that content area.

2. Note down 5–10 words you think you come across most frequently. Examine these words and consider if they might have different meanings in other content areas.

This chapter begins with a brief discussion of the creation of the Middle School Vocabulary Lists. Next, we look at the composition of these lists and see how they play out in sample paragraphs from content-area textbooks written at the middle school level, and we discuss the importance of the Middle School Vocabulary Lists for teachers and students. Finally, we offer some guidance in choosing the right time to focus on these words in the middle school classroom.

HOW WERE THE MIDDLE SCHOOL VOCABULARY LISTS CREATED?

Coxhead's (2000) AWL was the inspiration behind the development of Greene's (2008) Middle School Vocabulary Lists. The words on the AWL are incredibly useful for university students; after all, the list was derived from university-level reading materials. However, even though it was designed specifically for students in upper-level academia, the AWL has been used for students functioning well below that academic level. The thinking went something like this: if university students need to know these words, then teachers should make sure learners know them in high school. This seemed logical. Then, taking it one step further, the thinking was that, if students in high school need to know these words, then maybe teachers should focus on them in the middle grades, and maybe even the upper-elementary grades. Greene (2008) wondered whether the AWL was appropriate for middle school students, or whether there was a word list more useful for these students and their teachers. With these questions in mind, Greene used Coxhead's (2000) methodology to identify the academic words that middle school students need to know.

Greene began by collecting 109 textbooks written for Grades 6, 7, and 8, focusing on the content areas of English grammar and writing, health, mathematics, science, and social studies/history. These texts were scanned and then compiled to create the Middle School Content-Area Textbook (MS-CAT) Corpus. Greene then organized the MS-CAT Corpus into subcorpora representing each of the five content areas. From there, Greene used Range 1.32 (Heatley, Nation, & Coxhead, 2002) to identify the presence of GSL words (West, 1953) and AWL words contained in the MS-CAT Corpus and in each of the subcorpora. A final step included the identification of the most frequently occurring words in the subcorpora that were not a part of the GSL or the AWL. The identified words that met preset criteria for frequency and range are those that are included on each of the content-area lists of the Middle School Vocabulary Lists. A full description of the methodology used in this study is included in Appendix B of this book.

We have just provided a brief description of how the Middle School Vocabulary Lists were created. Next we will look at the most frequently occurring word families in each of these lists.

WHAT KINDS OF WORDS ARE INCLUDED IN THE MIDDLE SCHOOL VOCABULARY LISTS?

For a good conceptualization of how different categories of vocabulary work together in middle school texts, review Table 2.1, which shows the percentage of text coverage in each content area by the GSL (West, 1953) and each of the Middle School Vocabulary Lists. The first column demonstrates that the words on the GSL are doing a great deal of work in these

Table 2.1. Coverage of the content-area subcorpora by the General Service List and the Middle School Vocabulary Lists (%)

Content area subcorpora	General Service List[a]	Middle School Vocabulary List	Total
English grammar and writing	82.14	6.83	88.97
Health	82.73	8.70	91.43
Mathematics	79.64	9.29	88.93
Science	79.09	10.17	89.26
Social studies and history	77.91	5.83	83.74

[a]West (1953).

texts; their coverage hovers in the 82%–83% range for English grammar and writing as well as health, approximately 80% in mathematics and science, and approximately 78% in social studies and history. Coxhead (2000) found that GSL words represented about 76% of her university-level written Academic Corpus. When these numbers are compared, it is clear that middle school texts contain more GSL words than university-level texts. The second column in Table 2.1 shows the text coverage of the Middle School Vocabulary Lists, and the third column shows the total text coverage, which ranges right around the 90% mark for all content areas with the exception of social studies and history. Proper nouns play a large role in social studies and history texts, and this is one reason for lower text coverage. We discuss this more fully later in this chapter.

In Table 2.2 we present the top 20 word families contained on each of the Middle School Vocabulary Lists. A word family includes stems plus all affixes. So, for example, the word family for *benefit* would include these word family members: beneficial, beneficiary, beneficiaries, benefited, benefiting, and benefits. Thinking back to the discussion of categorization of vocabulary in Chapter 1, notice the presence of academic and technical words in each of these lists (e.g., *guidelines, hypothesis, geography, positive*). As noted in Chapter 1, Coxhead (2000) described academic words as having some key characteristics. First, they are not part of high-frequency vocabulary; second, they occur frequently in academic texts across content areas but not so frequently in other kinds of texts; and finally, they tend to support instructional topics contained in the text, but they do not actually represent those topics. Technical words, on the other hand, are those that are important to know because they occur frequently within a specific content area and they are directly related to the topics of that content area.

Table 2.2. The 20 most frequently occurring word families from each of the Middle School Vocabulary Lists

Middle School English Grammar and Writing List	Middle School Health List	Middle School Mathematics List	Middle School Science List	Middle School Social Studies and History List
pronoun	drug	equate	energy	chapter
phrase	physical	graph	cell	economy
adjective	alcohol	area	chapter	section
paragraph	stress	fraction	organism	region
topic	goal	chapter	atom	culture
adverb	teen	data	chemical	area
clause	affect	triangle	area	create
identify	emotion	percent	data	constitute
chapter	healthful	decimal	section	major
compound	injure	factor	element	congress
preposition	adult	mathematics	concept	identify
modify	chapter	meter	process	source
predicate	conflict	estimate	react	locate
revise	infect	rectangle	volcano	revolution
comma	muscle	subtract	occur	analyze
create	cell	integer	layer	geography
draft	concept	vary	structure	civil
essay	identify	sum	carbon	goods
tense	communicate	algebra	affect	issue
singular	cancer	function	meter	affect

One thing to keep in mind when looking at the words in Table 2.2 is that there is some representation of words across content areas. The word *chapter* is present on all five lists. Is this something you could have easily predicted, given that books with chapters make up the MS-CAT Corpus, or is it a surprise for you to learn? Words such as *create*, *affect*, and *identify* appear on multiple lists and can be considered truly academic in nature. On the other hand, there are words in each list that appear only in one content area (e.g., *adjective* and *adverb* in English grammar and writing; *equation, decimal,* and *percent* in mathematics), and these are clearly technical words within their content areas.

In addition, note how differences in words' meanings are represented in the various content areas. What is the difference between a *chemical process* in science and the *writing process*? Is there a difference between a geographical *area* in history and the *areas* described in mathematics or science? Seeing words laid out in this way helps in building connections between words and their various meanings across content areas.

Now that we have identified the kinds of words contained on the Middle School Vocabulary Lists, in the next section we look at how they are included in the running text of content-area textbooks.

HOW ARE MIDDLE SCHOOL VOCABULARY LIST WORDS INTEGRATED IN CONTENT-AREA TEXTBOOKS?

In this section, sample paragraphs from middle school content-area textbooks are examined, and the different kinds of vocabulary described in Chapter 1 are demonstrated as they are found in the texts.

English Grammar and Writing

The following paragraphs are taken from an eighth-grade grammar and writing textbook. Words appearing on the Middle School English Grammar and Writing Vocabulary List are underlined, and GSL words are bolded. Italicized words do not appear on either of these lists.

> Summarizing **means taking the main points of a written passage and** rewriting **them in a short account. You can do this by leaving out** *nonessential* **details and using your own words to make connections between the ideas and details. The** summary **should be about one-third as long as the original. The example below is a** summary **of the** professional **model on page 524.**
>
> **When you are doing** research **for a paper, you will be writing a number of note cards. These cards contain the ideas and information that will form the basis of your paper. Use a different card for each idea,** quotation, **or** statistic. **Give each card a heading that describes the note. Be sure to write the** source **information on the card. As you prepare to write your paper, you will need to organize the cards around** specific **points in your paper.** (McDougal Littel, 2001, pp. 525–526)

These two paragraphs contain 72 different word families. Of these, 64 are part of the GSL and eight are from the Middle School English Grammar and Writing Vocabulary List. Together, the words from these lists represent nearly 100% of the words in these two paragraphs (only one word, *nonessential,* is not included), which demonstrates how important the knowledge of the words on these lists is for middle school students required to read and learn from English grammar and writing textbooks.

Health

The following paragraphs are from an eighth-grade health textbook and demonstrate how the words on the GSL and the Middle School Health Vocabulary List are represented in the health subcorpus. Middle School Health Vocabulary List words are underlined, words from the GSL are bolded, and words that are not on either list are italicized.

> **Many** infections **are caused by** germs **called** viruses. **A** virus **is an extremely small particle that** consists **of an outer shell and** genetic **material. Unlike** bacteria, viruses **cannot reproduce by themselves. The only thing a** virus **can do is** attach **to and enter a host** cell. **It then takes over that host** cell's **machinery to make more** viruses. **Most scientists agree that** viruses **are not living** organisms **because** viruses **cannot reproduce outside of a host**.
>
> **The** symptoms **of a** viral infection vary **and may include** nasal congestion **and a sore throat, as in a cold, or body aches and fever, as in the** flu. Medi-cations **are now** available **to fight certain** viral infections, **such as** herpes **and** HIV/AIDS. **However, many of these** medications, **especially those used to treat** HIV, **have very unpleasant side effects. Today, many people are** vac-cinated **to prevent them from getting certain** viral infections. (Holt, Rinehart, and Winston, 2005, p. 433)

These two paragraphs contain 88 word families; of these, 68 are part of the GSL and 12 are part of the Middle School Health Vocabulary List (e.g., *virus, viral, viruses*). The interesting thing about these two paragraphs is the eight words that are not present on either list (e.g., *HIV, medications, congestion, genetic, herpes, nasal, organisms, vaccinated*). Chapter 1 discussed the idea of low-frequency vocabulary, and these words are examples of the low-frequency vocabulary in middle school health textbooks. Chapter 1 also explained how sometimes low-frequency vocabulary might also be technical vocabulary, and these words demonstrate that idea very nicely. Middle school health students are expected to know words such as *nasal congestion* and *vaccinated*; however, these words did not occur frequently enough throughout the health subcorpus to make the final list. As always, teachers need to make instructional decisions based on their students' specific needs. Any time teachers see technical words such as those that do not appear on any list, they can always do a simple thumbs-up/thumbs-down assessment to determine whether students know these words, and then decide whether their meanings need to be included in instruction.

Mathematics

The following paragraphs are taken from an eighth-grade mathematics textbook. GSL words are bolded and Middle School Mathematics Vocabulary List words are underlined. Italicized words are not present on either list.

> **A relation is a set of ordered pairs that relates an** input **to an** output. **A relation can be written as a set of ordered pairs or by using an** input–output

table. A relation is a <u>function</u> if for each <u>input</u> there is exactly one <u>output</u>. In a <u>function</u>, you can say that the <u>output</u> is the <u>function</u> of the <u>input</u>.

The <u>domain</u> of a <u>function</u> is the set of all possible <u>input</u> values. The <u>range</u> of a <u>function</u> is the set of all possible <u>output</u> values. A <u>function</u> rule <u>assigns</u> each number in the <u>domain</u> to exactly one number in the <u>range</u>.

A <u>sequence</u> is an ordered list of numbers. It is a special type of <u>function</u> whose <u>domain</u> includes only <u>positive integers</u> such as 1, 2, 3, and so on. Each <u>sequence</u> is made up of n numbers, or terms, and the value of each term is A. In an <u>arithmetic sequence</u>, the difference between *consecutive* terms is <u>constant</u>. Its <u>function</u> rule has the form A = an + b. (Larson, Boswell, Kanold, & Stiff, 2007, pp. 583–585)

These paragraphs contain 63 different word families. Of these, 51 word families are part of the GSL and 11 are part of the Middle School Mathematics Vocabulary List. All but one word *(consecutive)* is either part of the GSL or the Middle School Mathematics Vocabulary List, which is very good coverage, indeed!

One interesting thing to note is the amount of repetition of the Middle School Mathematics Vocabulary List words in those three paragraphs alone. For example, the word *function* occurs eight times, *input* and *output* each occur four times, and *domain* and *sequence* each occur three times. This helps to illustrate the role word frequency plays when developing a word list.

Science

The following paragraphs come from a physical science text written for eighth-grade students and demonstrate how the Middle School Science Vocabulary List and the GSL cover these two paragraphs. Once again, all of the GSL words are bolded and the words on the Middle School Science Vocabulary List are underlined. Italicized words do not appear on either list.

<u>Energy</u> **changes from one form to another, but it cannot be** <u>created</u> **or destroyed. All the changes you see around you depend on** <u>energy</u>. <u>Energy</u>, **in fact, means the ability to cause change. Using** <u>energy</u> **means changing** <u>energy</u>. **For example, you have seen electric** <u>energy</u> **changing into light, heat, sound, and mechanical** <u>energy</u> **in** *household appliances*. <u>Fuels</u> **like wood, coal, and oil contain** <u>chemical energy</u> **that produces heat when burned.**

<u>Energy</u> **can be** <u>converted</u> **into forms that can be used for** <u>specific</u> **purposes. During the** <u>conversion</u>, **some of the original** <u>energy</u> **is** <u>converted</u> **into unwanted or unusable forms. For example, when a power plant** <u>converts</u> <u>energy</u> **of falling water into electricity, some of the** <u>energy</u> **is lost to** <u>friction</u> **and sound. But** <u>energy</u> **is never** <u>created</u> **or destroyed, no matter how often it changes form. This fact is known as the law of** <u>conservation</u> **of** <u>energy.</u> (McDougal Littell, 2007, p. CA15)

These paragraphs contain words from 75 word families. Of these, 64 families are part of the GSL and eight are part of the Middle School Science Vocabulary List. The frequency of the word *energy* is immediately apparent; *energy* is the single most frequently occurring academic word in the Middle School Science Vocabulary List. In these two paragraphs, *energy* appears 14 times and represents more than 12% of the running text of the paragraphs.

A second point is the nature of the other words contained in the paragraph. The words *household* and *appliances* are part of the first paragraph, and when viewed in relation to all of the underlined words (e.g., *energy, friction, convert, create*), it becomes clear how different academic and technical words are from everyday words.

Social Studies and History

The two paragraphs in the following excerpt come from an American history textbook written for students in Grades 6–8. The underlined terms are from the Middle School Social Studies and History Vocabulary List, and bold indicates that a word is on the GSL. Words that are not part of either list are in italics.

> In <u>response</u> to the *Virginia* **Plan, New** *Jersey* <u>delegate</u> *William Paterson* **presented an** <u>alternative</u> **on June** 15. **The New** *Jersey* **Plan called for a** <u>legislature</u> **with only one house. In it, each state would have one vote. In providing equal representation to each state, the New** *Jersey* **Plan was** <u>similar</u> **to the Articles of** *Confederation.*
>
> **Even though the New** *Jersey* **Plan gave the** <u>legislature</u> **the power to** <u>regulate</u> **trade and to raise money by taxing foreign** <u>goods,</u> **it did not offer the broad powers proposed by the** *Virginia* **Plan. The** <u>delegates</u> **voted on these two plans on June** 19. **The** *Virginia* **Plan won and became the** <u>framework</u> **for** <u>drafting</u> **the** <u>Constitution.</u> (McDougal Littell, 2006, pp. 231–232)

Think of all of the people and places mentioned in social studies and history textbooks. These texts contain a large number of proper nouns, which were purposely excluded from the Middle School Social Studies and History Vocabulary List. The points made about categorizing proper nouns in Chapter 1 are illustrated quite nicely in these paragraphs. First, these terms contain high-frequency vocabulary (e.g., *new, plan*). In addition, terms such as the *New Jersey Plan* and the *Virginia Plan* refer to formal plans that delegates considered when drafting the U.S. Constitution, so students would need to conceptualize them differently than they would the names of the states of *New Jersey* and *Virginia*.

This section and subsections demonstrated how words on the Middle School Vocabulary Lists and the GSL (West, 1953) are integrated into content-area textbooks. The next section discusses the reasons why these lists are important for middle school teachers and students.

WHY ARE THE MIDDLE SCHOOL VOCABULARY LISTS IMPORTANT FOR MIDDLE SCHOOL TEACHERS AND STUDENTS?

Generally speaking, a good word list is one that represents (in terms of actual text coverage) exactly what it says it represents, but it does not contain so many words that it makes using the word list unmanageable. It is clear in the analyses described in the previous section that the Middle School Vocabulary Lists are useful lists for middle-grades teachers and their students, because they target the academic vocabulary these students will encounter in their textbooks and will be expected to use in spoken and written responses to their reading. Table 2.1 showed the high levels of text coverage students will reach by adding these words to their high-frequency vocabulary.

Coxhead (2000) described the AWL as a roadmap for students pursuing work at the university level, in that knowing those words would assist in making their coursework more manageable. The same can be said for middle school students who are required to read and learn from their course texts, as well as to use academic language in their speaking and writing. The Middle School Vocabulary Lists contain fewer words than the AWL, and yet they still provide good coverage of middle school textbooks. Students can use the lists to set and prioritize vocabulary learning goals for themselves. Teachers can use these lists to design instructional experiences that help students focus on the academic vocabulary they need to recognize and use every day.

SUMMARY

This chapter walked readers through the development of a corpus of middle school texts and the creation of word lists derived from this corpus. It demonstrated how the different categories of words are represented in five content areas; it also identified the most frequently occurring words from each of the Middle School Vocabulary Lists and demonstrated how the words on these lists show up in sample paragraphs from course texts used by middle school students. The next chapter will focus on developing a plan for vocabulary instruction in content-area classrooms, as well as provide research-based vocabulary teaching activities that teachers can use every day with middle school students.

DISCUSSION QUESTIONS

1. Return to the list of content-area words you noted in the Anticipation Activity at the beginning of this chapter. Now return to the top 20 lists discussed in the chapter and check your list against its corresponding content-area list. How accurate was your list?

2. This chapter looked at the development of a textbook corpus of middle school texts and the results of various word lists over that corpus. What do you think the coverage would be if we collected a corpus of spoken middle school texts instead of writing? How much

do you think these words from writing get used in speaking in your classroom?

3. What surprised you in this chapter with regard to the Middle School Vocabulary Lists?

4. What coverage of other texts might you predict the Middle School Vocabulary Lists to have? For example, what about newspapers, magazines, or other kinds of texts?

5. What are some of the challenges for teachers when it comes to working with tools such as the Middle School Vocabulary Lists?

6. How might you consider using the Middle School Vocabulary Lists in your classroom?

Planning for Integrating the Middle School Vocabulary Lists into Classroom Instruction

ANTICIPATION ACTIVITY

1. What principles do you follow when selecting and practicing vocabulary in your classrooms?

2. What are your responsibilities as a teacher when focusing on vocabulary in your classroom? What are your students' responsibilities?

3. What does the term *word consciousness* mean to you? What does it mean to your students and to your classroom?

"You can lead a horse to water, but you cannot make him drink": what this proverb means is that, in the end, people (including students) do what they want to do, not what others want them to do. What does this have to do with academic vocabulary? This proverb points to the idea of *intrinsic motivation* (see Guthrie & Wigfield [2000] for a full discussion of this idea) and to the creation of a classroom that assists students in forging a desire to learn about new words and the confidence to use their expanding vocabularies in their own schoolwork. In other words, teachers need to create an environment in which students want to drink from the pool of vocabulary knowledge offered to them. Vocabulary scholars

31

refer to this desire as *word consciousness* (Graves, 2006; Scott, Skobel, & Wells, 2008).

In this chapter, we discuss some really big ideas, such as word consciousness, as well as five principles for teaching and learning vocabulary (Nation, 2013). Then, with these big ideas in mind, we describe Nation's (2007) four strands for vocabulary instruction within the larger contexts of content-area instruction, building academic language using the Middle School Vocabulary Lists and this idea of word consciousness.

WHAT IS MEANT BY "WORD CONSCIOUSNESS"?

Students, as well as teachers, have responsibilities in the word-learning process, and Nation (2008) provides an excellent discussion of students' and teachers' jobs in this process. Teachers' responsibilities consist of planning, strategies instruction, testing, and teaching. Students' responsibilities are to use language, to participate in deliberate learning, and to take control of their own learning. The main point to take away from this discussion is the idea that building vocabulary knowledge is a two-way street, an idea that is not often specifically addressed in the literature. Many times, students need extra encouragement to do their jobs as vocabulary learners, and a teacher's job is to provide such encouragement through the creation of a word-conscious classroom.

There are whole books and sections of books devoted to the idea of word consciousness. These texts describe word-conscious students as having *metacognitive knowledge* (an ability to think about what they know), *metalinguistic knowledge* (an ability to think about language), and an *affective stance* toward words (a strong appreciation for words, enjoyment in learning about them, and an understanding of the power that comes with using them). Refer to Chapter 6 of Graves (2006), and the first chapter in Scott et al. (2008) for in-depth discussions of these ideas. Classrooms that promote word consciousness are those that assist students in developing these three components and make vocabulary learning both interesting and fun. We will develop these ideas throughout this chapter.

In this section, we described both the teachers' and students' jobs in the word-learning process and how this is related to the idea of word consciousness. In the next section, we explain how we can prioritize the words on the Middle School Vocabulary Lists.

HOW CAN TEACHERS SET PRIORITIES FOR FOCUSING ON SPECIFIC WORDS?

There are five principles to keep in mind for prioritizing vocabulary instruction: 1) the frequency principle, 2) the repetition principle, 3) the principle of spaced retrieval, 4) the principle of avoiding interference, and

5) the generation principle (Coxhead, 2006; Nation, 2013). We discuss each of these in turn in the following subsections.

The Frequency Principle

Frequency matters when planning vocabulary instruction. Teaching words that occur frequently and provide students with access to their texts has been recommended by leading scholars (National Institute of Child Health and Human Development, 2000; Snow, Lawrence, & White, 2009). By middle school, teachers can reasonably expect that students' oral vocabularies will be much larger than the 2,000 word families on the GSL (West, 1953). Teachers usually also expect that students will know how to read and write these words; however, students with special needs or new immigrants who are in the early stages of learning English may not. We illustrated the power of the words on the GSL and the coverage they provide in both narrative and expository texts in Chapter 1, so it is clear how important it is for all students to have control of these words and their meanings.

In Chapter 5, we discuss specific assessments that teachers can use to find out how many words their students know, and those assessments can assist in making an initial instructional decision. If students know the words on the GSL, then there is no need to waste time teaching those words, and the class can begin studying words on the Middle School Vocabulary Lists. However, if students do not have that foundational vocabulary in place, then the class will need to spend time focusing on high-frequency vocabulary (Graves, 2006). When the students are ready to focus attention on learning academic vocabulary, the teacher can use frequency again in making instructional decisions (Coxhead, 2006). Table 2.2 lists the 20 most frequently occurring word families on each of the Middle School Vocabulary Lists. The complete versions of these lists can be found in Appendix A. They are organized by their frequency in middle school textbooks, which will assist teachers in making decisions about the words they should focus on first.

The Repetition Principle

Students need to encounter new words over and over again in order to fully learn them. An important part of developing students' word consciousness is to be transparent about why repetition is important. Students need to know that the more they interact with words through reading and listening, the better they will be at using those words in their speaking and writing (Coxhead, 2006; Graves, 2006; Marzano, 2004; Snow et al., 2009).

When teachers consider words to target, they should make sure they are recycling words they have focused on earlier. Coxhead (2006) shares some key ideas for teachers to keep in mind when considering how they might do this:

1. Ensure that students interact with these words in a wide range of contexts over time. This means that students need opportunities to re-encounter these words through listening and reading as well as using them when speaking and writing.

2. Consider the time in between these repetitions so that students have time to absorb word meanings (see the principle of spaced retrieval in the next subsection).

3. Help students notice target words the class has focused on earlier when they hear them and read them. Refer to them specifically when using them during instruction, and encourage students to highlight words they have worked with when they see them in text.

4. Reuse the same text or use related texts containing the same vocabulary throughout various instructional activities.

5. Require students to use target words in small-group and whole-class discussions as well as in classroom writing tasks. In other words, students need to be held accountable for using the words that were targeted last week or last month as they move forward through the year in order to internalize their meanings and usage patterns.

The Principle of Spaced Retrieval

When students are able to pull a word's form or meaning from their memory, they are retrieving that word. The more times a learner retrieves a word from memory, the stronger the connection between the word and its meaning (Coxhead, 2006; Graves, 2006). This idea of retrieval works hand in hand with repetition. Teachers should provide learners with many repetitions of a new word when that word is introduced, making sure that those repetitions are spaced so that learners do not have time to forget them.

Students who are developing word consciousness need to understand how important it is to retrieve words from their memories over and over again. One great way to do this is to incorporate vocabulary cards in instructional events, as discussed more fully in Chapter 4.

The Principle of Avoiding Interference

Nation (2000, 2013) explained that it is not a good idea to teach lexically related words, such as words with similar forms (e.g., *affect* and *effect*), synonyms (e.g., *create* and *construct*), or antonyms (e.g., *exclude* and *include*), at the same time, especially if the target words are completely new to the learner. Teachers often argue this point, stating that they learned these kinds of words together with no harm done. However, the problem with doing so is that it often results in confusion for the learner that can last for a long time. For example, we both experienced this type of confusion learning the meanings of the words *hegemony* and *misogyny*. Both words were new to us when we first encountered them, and their forms were somewhat similar, and for these reasons their meanings were always muddled together, because they were initially presented to us in the same context. When planning to teach words that are lexically related, teachers should make sure students have a good understanding of the first word, and then introduce the second word at a later date.

However, textbooks often present lexically related items at the same time, so sometimes there is no way around this. For this reason, teachers and students need to be aware of this idea of interference so that everyone is working to avoid confusion. One way to do this is using Semantic Feature Analysis, which we describe in Chapter 4.

The Generation Principle

Students need opportunities to encounter and use new words in different contexts (Coxhead, 2006; Snow et al., 2009). Nation (2013) states that these encounters need to involve "the creative use" (p. 110) of words. Here is an example: In science class, the word *buoyant* can describe an object's ability to float, but the word *buoyant* can also be used to describe a positive feeling (i.e., she is feeling remarkably *buoyant* today). This metaphorical extension of word meaning is only one example of creative use; others can be changes in collocational (the idea that words habitually co-occur [Hunston, 2002, p. 12; Sinclair, 1991, p. 170], e.g., collocates of the word *process* include *complete, complicated, constant, democratic,* and *due*), contextual, semantic, or grammatical uses of the word. When a student is able to use a word in speaking or writing in a way that is different from the way it was used in a source text, it is clear that the student is using that word in a creative way. Teachers can assist students in developing creativity in word use by integrating levels of creativity into their own speaking, as well as highlighting different usage patterns as they are encountered in written text. Teachers also need to provide students with opportunities to use words creatively in their own speaking and writing activities.

In this section we discussed five principles to keep in mind when prioritizing vocabulary instruction. In the next section, we share four strands for vocabulary instruction described by Nation (2007) and explain how these strands can play out in reading, writing, speaking, and listening activities.

WHAT ARE NATION'S FOUR STRANDS FOR VOCABULARY INSTRUCTION?

Through their education courses and professional development opportunities, most teachers have likely become familiar with many different activities and strategies for teaching and learning vocabulary; however, these strategies are, more often than not, limited to developing students' understandings of a target word's forms, meanings, and functions. While these are important for students to know, they represent only one instructional strand in a balanced vocabulary program.

Nation (2007) describes four instructional strands that should be evenly balanced to maximize effectiveness when focusing on words from the Middle School Vocabulary Lists. These strands are 1) meaning-focused input (learning target vocabulary through reading and listening), 2) meaning-focused output (learning target vocabulary through writing and speaking), 3) language-focused learning (learning the pronunciation, spelling, morphology, grammar-use patterns, and other elements of target vocabulary), and 4) fluency (the ability to use target vocabulary with speed and accuracy in reading, writing, speaking, and listening). The activities of learning vocabulary through reading, writing, speaking, and listening are all meaning based. The emphasis in these activities should be on students understanding and learning from what they hear and read as well as communicating what they have learned through speaking and writing. Language-focused learning, on the other hand, is direct learning, and its focus is on various features of words rather than on their meanings. Fluency development activities put it all together; students integrate their understandings of language features and meanings when they are encouraged to use that language in timed reading, writing, speaking, and listening activities. Once teachers have decided which words they will target for instruction, they should make certain that learning activities incorporate each of these strands evenly (see Nation, 2007, pp. 2–7 for a full discussion of these ideas).

How Do These Strands Relate to Curriculum, the Middle School Vocabulary Lists, and the Vocabulary Classroom?

Throughout their careers, teachers spend considerable time observing classroom instruction. In the next subsections, we share some of the patterns we have noticed and demonstrate how they can affect meaning-focused input, meaning-focused output, language-focused learning, and fluency.

Learning Academic Vocabulary Through Reading and Listening (Meaning-Focused Input)

The first pattern we have noticed during observations of content-area classrooms is that students are not always required to read their textbooks. Teachers have many reasons for this, ranging from lack of time to the belief that students cannot actually read their textbooks. The difficulty, however, is that when students are not reading their course texts, they are deprived of opportunities to encounter academic and technical words through meaning-focused input. The words on the Middle School Vocabulary Lists occur frequently throughout middle school textbooks.

In Chapter 2 we illustrated this point by showing how the words on these lists occur in passages from content-area textbooks. We know students will repeatedly encounter these words when reading textbooks; therefore, it is critically important that students be required to use their textbooks during classroom activities. If students struggle with the academic language or ideas in their grade-level textbooks, Coxhead, Stevens, and Tinkle (2010) suggested that they might benefit from reading about that topic in an earlier-grade text, which would allow them to explore ideas and language in an easier version before reading the more difficult (grade-level) version.

Our second observation is that a great deal of instructional time in content-area classrooms is spent discussing whatever topic is on the curriculum's instructional calendar at any given moment. These events provide a great opportunity for students to be exposed to academic and technical words through listening, which is meaning-focused input. Teachers do a great job of using technical terms in their lectures (actually, there is not any real way around this), but they do not always use supportive academic words in these events; instead, they often rely on high-frequency vocabulary to communicate ideas.

Keeping in mind the principles of repetition and spaced retrieval, one idea to support word consciousness is for teachers to be very purposeful about including appropriate academic and technical words from the Middle School Vocabulary Lists during instructional events and to be transparent about doing so. When students hear teachers repeatedly using academic language, they receive meaning-focused input through listening as well as being provided opportunities to retrieve target words' meanings from memory.

One good way for teachers to know how often they are indeed using academic language in the classroom is to tape record themselves for 15 minutes and note down the academic words used during that time. They might be surprised by the result! If teachers want to be more purposeful about incorporating target words as they talk, here are some suggestions. First, plan the words to target—do not wing it! Note down several key phrases that can be used repeatedly throughout the class period and keep track of the number of times they were used.

Another suggestion is to display preplanned key phrases on a SMART Board or on a PowerPoint using an overhead projector. Tell students in advance that you will be using these phrases during your time together. Engage your students in your plan by asking them to keep track of the number of times you used key phrases and then having a discussion about your usage afterwards. Incorporating this practice will provide students with meaning-focused input. At the same time, you will be modeling the effort it takes to use academic language, so do not be surprised when your students start using those key phrases themselves!

Learning Academic Vocabulary Through Writing and Speaking (Meaning-Focused Output)

As we shared in our previous section, the principles of repetition and spaced retrieval are important in assisting students' developing word knowledge. These principles speak directly to the idea of meaning-focused output. When we consider meaning-focused output in our classrooms, the idea of writing and speaking for meaning (i.e., using academic language to communicate new knowledge and understanding) should be a central core of classroom activities.

During our observations of content-area classrooms, we have noticed that, although teachers may be using academic language as they teach (providing meaning-focused input), students are not required to use that academic language during their classroom speaking and writing tasks, so they are missing opportunities for meaning-focused output. As an example, a common feature of a middle school classroom is a word wall containing target academic and technical vocabulary from previous and current instruction, with the expectation that if the words are displayed, students will use them. Unfortunately, this does not happen serendipitously. Given the importance of meaning-focused output, students need to become more purposeful about incorporating the words from the Middle School Vocabulary Lists in their classroom discussions about the topics they are studying as well as in their written responses to text, and teachers need to set classroom expectations so that students are required to do so.

Learning the Pronunciation, Spelling, Morphology, Grammar-Use Patterns, and Other Elements of Academic Vocabulary (Language-Focused Learning)

There are many aspects of knowing a word, and we discuss these in detail in Chapter 5. In addition to knowing the meaning of a word, students also need to know about its form and usage patterns. This means that teachers need to include activities that focus on pronunciation, spelling, morphology, and grammar use as part of their academic language instruction. These aspects of vocabulary learning tend to be incremental in nature, which means that students will not learn all of this information at the same time (Schmitt, 2010). For this reason, teachers spend a lot of time directly teaching these concepts, and that is important; however, keep in mind that language-focused learning is only one of four strands and needs to be evenly balanced with the others. We include activities in Chapter 4 to assist teachers in providing language-focused learning in the classroom.

Developing the Ability to Use Academic Vocabulary with Speed and Accuracy in Reading, Writing, Speaking, and Listening (Fluency)

Fluency activities are those that provide students opportunities to develop their speed and accuracy in using target vocabulary. This is important, because students only fully know a word when they can use it accurately and without hesitation when speaking and writing, as well as recognize and understand it immediately when they hear it or read it. Students need to fluently use the words on the Middle School Vocabulary Lists, and we share activities for developing target word fluency in Chapter 4.

SUMMARY

In this chapter we described Nation's (2001, 2007, 2013) five principles and four strands for teaching and learning vocabulary and described how these principles can play out in a balanced program of vocabulary instruction that includes meaning-focused input and output, language-focused learning, and fluency practice, all within the larger idea of word consciousness. In Chapter 4 we outline various vocabulary learning activities that incorporate these four strands.

DISCUSSION QUESTIONS

1. Rank the principles from Nation (2007) in terms of importance to you as a teacher. Why have you ranked them this way? What influence might these principles have on your vocabulary teaching?

2. Consider the four strands in your planning for focusing on academic language and using the Middle School Vocabulary Lists. Which strands are already part of your planning and which will you focus on including in the future?

4

Activities that Focus on Middle School Vocabulary List Words

ANTICIPATION ACTIVITY

1. Think about how you focus on vocabulary in your classroom today. Note down three or four activities through which you help your students develop academic language.

2. Now consider the effectiveness of those activities based on your students' academic language use during speaking and writing. Are your students incorporating these words during speaking and writing activities? How often and how accurately are these words used?

When teachers help students focus on academic vocabulary in the classroom, students learn content at the same time (Alverman, Phelps, & Gillis, 2010), and the words on the Middle School Vocabulary Lists either represent the concepts students are learning (e.g., *region, culture*) or they help support those concepts (e.g., *adopt, consist*). It is important for students to have control of both the supportive terms and the technical terms contained on these lists, because when students recognize these words during reading or listening activities, and incorporate them in speaking and writing activities, as they are required to do under the CCSS, they are demonstrating their understanding of these concepts. The point is that focusing on these words will not take away from instruction time; rather, it makes better use of the time at hand.

In this chapter, we present 14 activities to help students focus on words from the Middle School Vocabulary Lists. Each of these activities provides learners with one or more of the instructional strands defined by Nation (2007; see Chapter 3 for a summary): meaning-focused input, meaning-focused output, language-focused learning, and practice developing fluency. The activities are organized according to their primary strand; however, we also indicate when they can be used in alignment with additional strands.

Using these activities in your vocabulary learning classroom will help you provide balance between these four strands. Additionally, when you incorporate these activities you will also provide vocabulary learning opportunities consistent with Nation's (2013) five principles for teaching and learning vocabulary, summarized in Chapter 3. Each activity includes a brief description and rationale for implementing it in the classroom, followed by a step-by-step outline of the activity. We also offer fix-ups to assist in modifying the strategy based on students' needs and make suggestions for extending vocabulary instruction to other vocabulary learning activities.

ACTIVITIES FOR PROVIDING MEANING-FOCUSED INPUT AND MEANING-FOCUSED OUTPUT

The activities in this section will assist students in learning new words through reading and listening.

JIGSAW READING

| Meaning-focused input | ☑ | Language-focused learning | ☐ |
| Meaning-focused output | ☑ | Developing fluency | ☐ |

WHAT IS IT?

Jigsaw reading (Slavin, 1996) is a type of split-information activity that requires students to read short texts or parts of a single text and become experts about the content they have read. Next they share what they have learned with others, through speaking and/or writing activities.

WHY DO IT?

Jigsaw reading provides students opportunities to do the following:

- Participate in cooperative learning groups.
- Learn content and target academic and technical vocabulary through reading and listening (meaning-focused input).
- Use target academic and technical vocabulary to share what they have learned through speaking and writing (meaning-focused output).

HOW TO IMPLEMENT

1. Decide how many groups you will have. As an example, a class of 24 students could have six groups of four students each.

2. Select text(s) for this activity. You may decide to break a single text into multiple sections (one section for each group) or select multiple texts on the same topic (one text for each group). Help students notice academic and technical words by highlighting those words within the text.

3. Prepare reading guides for your text selections to help students focus on the content and vocabulary contained in the selected texts.

4. Place students in expert groups. Within groups, number students 1, 2, 3, and 4. Expert group members should all receive the same text and copies of the reading guide.

5. Have students do the following:

   • Read independently using their reading guides as a support.

   • Work together as a group to complete their reading guides.

6. Have students move into sharing groups. All 1s are in a group, 2s are in a group, and so on.

7. Make sure each student has a blank copy of the other groups' reading guides. Have students do the following:

   • Take turns sharing what they learned in their expert groups, incorporating target academic and technical vocabulary in their responses.

   • Assist other group members in completing reading guides.

8. Finally, have students move back into their expert groups. Have students do the following:

   • Discuss what they learned during their sharing groups, using target academic vocabulary.

   • Work together to clarify misunderstandings.

9. Bring groups back to whole-class discussion. Students share what they have learned, using target academic vocabulary during the discussion.

10. Provide additional clarification and support as needed.

FIX-UPS

Make sure the text selections you make are on an appropriate reading level for struggling readers or ELLs. For more information about using graded readers in the classroom, Sonia Millett, at the University of Wellington, New Zealand, has published articles on this topic as well as graded versions of popular fiction on her web site (http://victoria.ac.nz/lals/about/staff/sonia-millett).

EXTENSIONS

Triple-Entry Vocabulary Journals Have students add to what they know about target academic and technical vocabulary in their triple-entry vocabulary journals (see subsection on triple-entry journals later in this chapter).

Quick Writing Have students complete a quick write (see subsection on quick writing later in this chapter) detailing what they have learned in this activity, using target academic vocabulary in their responses.

Other Projects Have students use what they have learned to support formal presentations and other research projects.

NARROW READING

| Meaning-focused input | ☑ | Language-focused learning | ☐ |
| Meaning-focused output | ☑ | Developing fluency | ☐ |

WHAT IS IT?

Narrow reading (Schmitt, 2000) is an activity during which students read multiple instructional-level texts written about the same topic.

WHY DO IT?

Narrow reading provides students opportunities to do the following:

- Increase background knowledge of a single topic.
- Synthesize their understanding of a topic across multiple texts.
- Learn content and target academic and technical vocabulary through reading and listening (meaning-focused input).
- Use target academic and technical vocabulary to share what they have learned through speaking and writing (meaning-focused output).

HOW TO IMPLEMENT

1. Select three to five different texts written about the same topic.
2. Choose target academic and technical words contained across the texts. Help students notice target academic and technical words by highlighting them in the text.
3. Prepare reading guides to support students reading the texts, helping students notice target vocabulary as well as content.
4. Have students do the following:
   - Independently read the texts, using their reading guides.
   - Work independently or in small groups to complete their reading guides.

5. Bring students to whole-class discussion. Have students share what they have learned, incorporating target academic vocabulary in their responses.

6. Provide additional clarification and support as needed.

FIX-UPS

Make sure that text selections are on an appropriate level for struggling readers and ELLs.

EXTENSIONS

Other Projects (e.g., research papers or presentations)   This is an excellent first step for a research paper or presentation, so learners can present the main ideas from their reading, add analysis of their own to the topic, and use the opportunity to practice the vocabulary they have encountered in the reading.

Quick Writing   Have students summarize what they have learned from the narrow reading activity in a quick write using target academic and technical vocabulary.

Vocabulary Cards   Have students create vocabulary cards for the target academic and technical vocabulary contained in their reading selections (see subsection on vocabulary cards later in this chapter).

Triple-Entry Vocabulary Journal   Have students add what they have learned about target academic and technical vocabulary words to their triple-entry vocabulary journals.

CLOSE READING

Meaning-focused input	☑	Language-focused learning	☐
Meaning-focused output	☑	Developing fluency	☐

WHAT IS IT?

Close reading describes reading activities during which readers read and reread sections of complex text with specific purposes guiding rereading events. Refer to Zwiers, O'Hara, and Pritchard (2014), Chapter 4, for a full discussion of close reading using complex informational texts.

WHY DO IT?

Repeated reading of sections of complex informational texts provides students opportunities to do the following:

- Understand key concepts contained in the text.
- Interpret the text in multiple ways.

- Develop critical reading skills.
- Gain new insights into already-known concepts.
- Learn content and target academic and technical vocabulary through reading and listening (meaning-focused input).
- Use target academic and technical vocabulary to share what they have learned through speaking and writing (meaning-focused output).

HOW TO IMPLEMENT

1. Determine a purpose for the activity (e.g., identifying and analyzing evidence contained in a text, interpreting a text from multiple points of view, developing increased understanding of content).
2. Select a text that meets your purpose.
3. Identify target academic and technical vocabulary contained in the text. Help students notice academic and technical words by highlighting them in the text.
4. Have students independently read the selected text.
5. Tell students what the purpose of the activity is. Provide a graphic organizer or reading guide to assist them in applying this purpose during rereading.
6. Have students work in pairs or small groups and do the following:
   - Reread the text selection with the purpose in mind.
   - Work together to complete their graphic organizers or reading guides.
   - Use their graphic organizers or reading guides to prepare a written response to the text, using target academic and technical vocabulary in their response.
7. Next, have two groups merge and have students share their written group responses with each other. Groups may revise their written responses based on what they learn in this segment.
8. Bring students together as a whole class and have them share what they have learned based on their purpose for reading. Students should use target academic or technical vocabulary during this discussion.
9. Provide additional clarification and support as needed.

FIX-UPS

Struggling readers and ELLs may benefit from paired reading of the selected text.

EXTENSIONS

4-3-2 for Fluency   Have students use what they have learned in this activity to prepare their 4-3-2 for Fluency (see subsection on 4-3-2 for

Fluency later in this chapter) talks using target academic and technical vocabulary.

Quick Writing   Have students summarize what they have learned in a quick write using target academic and technical words.

Vocabulary Cards   Have students create vocabulary cards for new academic or technical target vocabulary.

Triple-Entry Vocabulary Journal   Have students make an entry in their triple-entry vocabulary journals based on what they have learned about target academic or technical vocabulary.

CONCEPT MAP

| Meaning-focused input | ☑ | Language-focused learning | ☐ |
| Meaning-focused output | ☑ | Developing fluency | ☐ |

WHAT IS IT?

A concept map (semantic map) allows students to graphically demonstrate relationships between words. Concept maps were first introduced in the 1980s (Johnson & Pearson, 1984), and repeated research demonstrates that concept maps are a powerful tool for vocabulary learning (Baumann, Kame'enui, & Ash, 2003; Blachowicz & Fisher, 2000).

WHY DO IT?

Incorporating concept maps in your classroom will accomplish the following:

- Aid students in developing vocabulary knowledge at the same time they are learning content knowledge.
- Help students to see the connections between related words and concepts.
- Provide students with a visual representation of the text.
- Give support for oral and written communication.
- Learn content and target academic and technical vocabulary through reading and listening (meaning-focused input).
- Use target academic and technical vocabulary to share what they have learned through speaking and writing (meaning-focused output).

Figure 4.1 is a concept map incorporating Middle School Science Vocabulary List words contained in a chapter from a physical science text. Science Vocabulary List words used in the map are bolded.

HOW TO IMPLEMENT

1. Introduce concept maps by choosing a topic with which the class is familiar and developing a concept map for that topic on the

Concept map

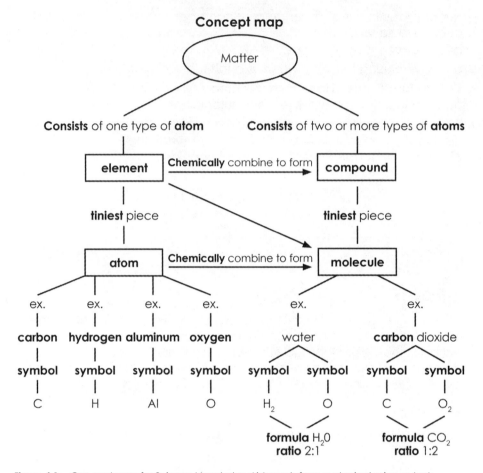

Figure 4.1. Concept map for Science Vocabulary List words from a physical science text.

board or an overhead projector. Provide your students opportunities to brainstorm ideas for the map and make connections between those ideas.

2. Once students are comfortable with the process, introduce a map related to the content you are teaching.

3. Begin with the main idea.

4. Add in target academic and technical vocabulary words.

5. Make connections between the academic and technical words using lines or arrows to demonstrate the relationships between the terms.

6. Demonstrate using the map to review the relationships between the terms, focusing on target academic vocabulary. This can be done by saying or writing a couple of sentences using target academic

and technical vocabulary based on the information in the map. The following are example sentences from Figure 4.1:

- Elements and compounds are two types of matter.
- Elements are made of one type of atom.
- Compounds are made of two or more types of atoms.

7. Have students volunteer to say or write their own sentences based on the concept map.

FIX-UPS

1. If students are overwhelmed with a full version of a concept map, break the map into smaller portions until students are comfortable with the process.

2. Students may have difficulty using the map to assist in speaking and writing about the topic, so be ready to step in and provide additional modeling and scaffolding as needed.

EXTENSIONS

Quick Writing   Have students use their concept map as a scaffold for writing about what they have learned.

4-3-2 for Fluency   Have students use their concept map as a scaffold for preparing their 4-3-2 for Fluency talks.

Word Sorts   Have students sort the words on their concept map according to their form, meaning, or function.

LANGUAGE-FOCUSED LEARNING ACTIVITIES

The activities in this section will assist students in learning the spelling, grammatical, and morphological features of academic words in addition to their meanings.

THE FRAYER MODEL

| Meaning-focused input | ☐ | Language-focused learning | ☑ |
| Meaning-focused output | ☐ | Developing fluency | ☐ |

WHAT IS IT?

The Frayer Model (Frayer, Frederick, & Klausmeier, 1969) uses a graphic organizer to help students explore deeper meanings of select words.

WHY DO IT?

The Frayer Model provides students opportunities to clarify their understanding of target academic vocabulary by performing the following tasks:

- Comparing and contrasting between a target word's essential and nonessential characteristics
- Identifying examples and nonexamples of the target word's meaning

HOW TO IMPLEMENT

1. Identify target words from your current instruction. For example, in a middle school American history chapter about Andrew Jackson's presidency, popular democracy, and conflicts over states' rights, students need a rich understanding of key terms in order to understand the content of the text (e.g., *compromise, democracy, issue, policy*).

2. Provide students with a Frayer Model graphic organizer (Figure 4.2). Frayer Model graphic organizers consist of four squares labeled *essential characteristics, nonessential characteristics, examples,* and *nonexamples*. The target word is placed in the center.

3. Display a copy of the graphic organizer on a SMART Board or on a PowerPoint using an overhead projector.

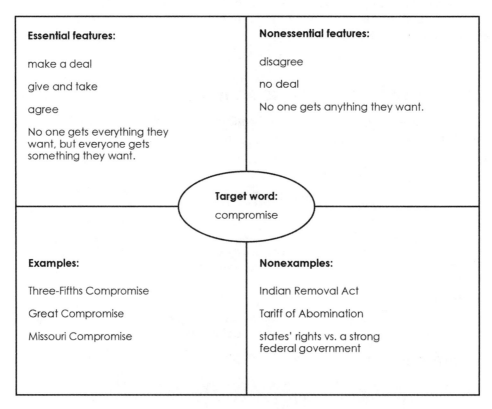

Essential features:

make a deal

give and take

agree

No one gets everything they want, but everyone gets something they want.

Nonessential features:

disagree

no deal

No one gets anything they want.

Target word:
compromise

Examples:

Three-Fifths Compromise

Great Compromise

Missouri Compromise

Nonexamples:

Indian Removal Act

Tariff of Abomination

states' rights vs. a strong federal government

Figure 4.2. Graphic organizer for the Frayer Model. (*Source:* Frayer, Frederick, & Klausmeier, 1969.)

4. Have students write the key term in the center of the graphic organizer.

5. Have students brainstorm ideas to complete each of the areas of the graphic organizer. Discuss students' ideas and record ideas on a SMART Board or on a PowerPoint using an overhead projector. Students should be able to make connections between essential features and examples and between nonessential features and nonexamples.

6. Have students complete their individual organizers while you are completing the displayed organizer.

7. Have students work with a partner and take turns describing the target word to each other using their graphic organizers as a guide.

FIX-UPS

• This strategy focuses on a single word's meaning, and it can take some time to complete. For this reason, we suggest that you limit this strategy to key concepts related to your current chapter.

• You can modify the category titles in each square to help your students focus on more specific ideas related to your content area.

• Depending upon individual student's developmental needs, you may need to provide explanations for some of the ideas presented in the class.

EXTENSIONS

Quick Writing   Have students summarize their understanding of the target word in a quick write.

Triple-Entry Journals   Before using the Frayer Model, have students describe their understanding of the target word in their triple-entry journals. After using the Frayer Model, have students add their new understandings to their entry.

Word Builder   Once students have an understanding of the target word from the Frayer Model, have them focus on the morphological variations of that word using the Word Builder activity (described later in this section).

WORD SORTS

| Meaning-focused input | ☐ | Language-focused learning | ☑ |
| Meaning-focused output | ☐ | Developing fluency | ☐ |

WHAT IS IT?

Word sorting (Gillett, Temple, & Crawford, 2004) is a hands-on activity allowing students to manipulate words into categories based on their meanings, relationships, forms, and functions.

WHY DO IT?

- Word sorts provide students with opportunities to compare and contrast, analyze word meanings, or analyze word form.
- You will never run out of ideas for categorizing word sorts—words can be sorted according to their form, meaning, or function.

HOW TO IMPLEMENT

1. Choose a topic for your word sort. Choose up to 20 academic words related to that topic.
2. Decide whether you want students to sort words into their own categories (open sort) or whether you want to pick the categories yourself (closed sort). There are ample possibilities for word sorts. We have listed several in the example later in this activity.
3. Model the sorting process for your students and explain the reasons for your sort.
5. Place students in small groups.
4. Provide groups with small pieces of paper or card stock. Have students do the following:
   - Write target words on paper or card stock.
   - Sort words into categories and record their sorts on a sheet of paper.
   - Volunteer to share their sorts with the class and explain the decisions they made when sorting the words into categories.

Example

Target words from physical science:

atom	hydrogen	C
element	aluminum	H
compound	oxygen	H_2
molecule	carbon dioxide	Al
symbol	water	O
carbon	formula	O_2

Possible sorts:

- Sort words by elements.
- Sort words by symbols.
- Match elements and symbols.
- Sort words into formulas for water and carbon dioxide.

FIX-UPS

- If students are new to word sorts, scaffold the process by choosing sorts for them (closed sorts). Once students become familiar with the process, they can begin to choose their own categories for their sorts (open sorts).

- Ensure students' success by providing additional modeling and guided practice as needed before allowing them to work independently.
- Consider your students' developmental level when selecting target words for word sorts.

EXTENSIONS

Quick Writing   Have students write about their word sorts in a quick write.

Concept Map   Once students have sorted words into categories, have them develop a concept map based on those categories.

Vocabulary Cards   Have students create vocabulary cards for the words in their word sort.

Semantic Feature Analysis   Have students complete a semantic feature analysis (see activity later in this chapter) to analyze the differences between words in each category.

TRIPLE-ENTRY VOCABULARY JOURNAL

| Meaning-focused input | ☐ | Language-focused learning | ☑ |
| Meaning-focused output | ☐ | Developing fluency | ☐ |

WHAT IS IT?

A triple-entry vocabulary journal is a variation of the dual-entry diary described by Berthoff (1981), which helps students focus specifically on word learning.

WHY DO IT?

When students complete triple-entry vocabulary journals, they have opportunities to accomplish the following:

- Make connections between word meanings across content areas and link word meanings to their own lives.
- Read, think about what they have read, and write about their thoughts.
- Build a personal record of word learning.

In addition, triple-entry vocabulary journals provide teachers opportunities to communicate with students individually via feedback on their entries.

HOW TO IMPLEMENT

1. Select a reasonable number of target words that appear in a current chapter. Choose words that occur frequently or are important

for understanding the text. The number of words you choose depends on the amount of time you have to work with them in class.

2. Provide students with a template for their triple-entry vocabulary journals (see Figure 4.3). The template should have three columns labeled *Target word, Sentence in text,* and *My thoughts*.

3. Model a sample entry in a triple-entry vocabulary journal for your students. Example:

Target word: *function*

Sentence in text: All of your body systems work together to make your body *function* properly.

My thoughts: Sometimes parties or school dances are called *functions*, and I know that in math a *function* can be a relationship between sets. But in this sentence, I think *function* means that my body is doing what it is supposed to be doing.

4. Have students complete their triple-entry vocabulary journals using the academic words you have selected.

5. Have students volunteer to share their thoughts with the class.

6. Review students' triple-entry vocabulary journals. Provide feedback and share some of your own thoughts. This final step is important, because it gives you a chance to check students' understanding of word meanings and provides you an opportunity to communicate with them individually. Do not be surprised when your students start responding to your responses!

Target word	Sentence in text	My thoughts

Figure 4.3. Template for triple-entry journals. (*Source:* Berthoff, 1981.)

FIX-UPS

- Consider your students' developmental level when planning to use this strategy. As an example, ELLs may benefit from using a bilingual dictionary to assist them, or they may require additional information from you. In either case, have students jot down some ideas about what they think the word might mean, then use additional resources to check their thoughts. They can write about that process in the *My thoughts* section in their triple-entry vocabulary journals.

- If your students seem to be struggling with the process, provide additional modeling and guidance as necessary.

- You can assign triple-entry vocabulary journal entries for homework or for independent practice once you feel confident that your students understand the process and can complete it on their own.

EXTENSIONS

Vocabulary Cards   Once students have developed ideas about word meanings through triple-entry vocabulary journals, they can create vocabulary cards using more formal definitions.

Word Chain   Have students do word chain activities (see activity on word chains later in this chapter) to explore additional morphological forms of the target word along with their meanings and uses.

VOCABULARY CARDS

Meaning-focused input	☐	Language-focused learning	☑
Meaning-focused output	☐	Developing fluency	☐

WHAT IS IT?

Vocabulary cards (Coxhead, 2006; Nation, 2013) are useful when introducing new academic words to your class. They contain information about the word's form and use on the front and definitional information on the back. Use three-by-five index cards or card stock with the front side divided into four squares for vocabulary cards (see Figures 4.4 and 4.5).

WHY DO IT?

When students develop vocabulary cards, they have opportunities to accomplish the following:

- Combine both verbal and visual information about a word.

- Create an easy-to-handle study tool; multiple cards can be stored in a box or gathered together in a rubber band so that students can easily refer back to them.

Academic word:	Part of speech: Word family members:
Use this word in a sentence:	Picture:

Figure 4.4. Vocabulary card (front).

Definition: Translation and/or cognate:

Figure 4.5. Vocabulary card (back).

- Find information about a word's form, meaning, and use—all in one place.
- Be responsible for the accuracy of the information on their cards.
- Retrieve a word's meaning from memory because the definition is on the back of the card.

HOW TO IMPLEMENT

1. Select a reasonable number of academic words related to the content you are teaching.

2. Use one of your selected words and model the development of a vocabulary card on a SMART Board or on a PowerPoint using an overhead projector. Write the target word in one square, word family members in another square, a sentence using the target word in the third square, and draw a picture about the word in the fourth square. Allow students to volunteer information that could be included on the vocabulary card.

3. Write a student-friendly definition on the back of the card, as an example.

4. Have students work in small groups.

5. Provide each group with index cards and one academic word.

6. Students work together to complete their vocabulary cards.

7. Have a volunteer from each group share their completed vocabulary card with the class.

8. Class members listen and record presented information onto additional vocabulary cards.

9. Monitor students' work throughout the activity and provide additional feedback and modeling when necessary.

FIX-UPS

- You can customize vocabulary cards for ELLs by incorporating additional useful information. Students can add details about pronunciation and word stress to the front of the card, and on the back they can add cognates or other translation information (Coxhead, 2006).

- Students may have difficulty coming up with their own definitions for a word. When this happens, scaffold their learning by providing access to student-friendly dictionaries (including bilingual dictionaries) or by referring them to the text.

EXTENSIONS

Word Chains Have students complete word chaining for form and use. Add the information they have learned to their vocabulary cards.

Cognate Strategy Have students identify true and false cognates for their target word (see activity on identifying and using cognates later in this chapter) and add that information to their vocabulary cards.

SEMANTIC FEATURE ANALYSIS

| Meaning-focused input | ☑ | Language-focused learning | ☑ |
| Meaning-focused output | ☑ | Developing fluency | ☐ |

WHAT IS IT?

Semantic feature analysis (Anders & Bos, 1986; Schmitt, 2000) involves using a graphic organizer to help students understand similarities and differences between different concepts and words.

WHY DO IT?

This strategy is especially effective when you must teach synonyms, antonyms, or words that share similar forms at the same time (see our discussion about the principal of avoiding interference in Chapter 3).

HOW TO IMPLEMENT

1. Identify target words from your current instruction. For example, in physical science, students are required to understand the similarities and differences between *physical changes* and *chemical changes*.

2. Prepare a graphic organizer like the one in Figure 4.6. Determine the features that are associated with each term and add those to the graphic organizer.

3. Display your graphic organizer on the board or an overhead projector.

4. Present the target terms to students. Point out their similarities in form and/or meaning and tell students that this activity will help them understand the differences between the two.

5. Have students volunteer to share whatever understandings they might have of the displayed terms (they may have no knowledge of your target words at this point, and that is okay).

	Change (alteration) in matter	Change (alteration) makes something new	Form is changed (altered) but it is still the same	Water changes to ice	Iron changes to rust
Physical change	+	-	+	+	-
Chemical change	+	+	-	-	+

Figure 4.6. Semantic feature analysis grid for physical and chemical changes in matter. (*Source:* Pittelman, 1986.)

5. Discuss the features on the graphic organizer with your students. Explain that these features may be related in some way to one or both of the target terms on your graphic organizer.

6. Have students do the following:

   • Read about these terms in a brief passage from their textbooks.

   • Place a plus symbol (+) in the corresponding box if the term and the feature are related.

   • Place a minus symbol (–) in the corresponding box if the term and the feature are not related; if they cannot find the answer in their text, they may put a question mark (?) in the corresponding box.

7. Discuss the results of students' analysis of target words and features, checking for accuracy and understanding.

FIX-UPS

If students are new to semantic feature analysis, work through this activity the first time as a whole class. Model your thinking as you read through the text and complete the graphic organizer. The second time, you can have students work in small groups or pairs, and the third time, allow them to do this activity independently.

EXTENSIONS

Quick Write   Have students describe the similarities and differences between the two terms using academic language in their responses.

Vocabulary Cards   Once students have completed semantic feature analysis, have them transfer what they have learned to individual vocabulary cards.

4-3-2 for Fluency   Have students use their semantic feature analysis graphic organizers to support short talks about what they have learned.

IDENTIFYING AND USING COGNATES

| Meaning-focused input | ☐ | Language-focused learning | ☑ |
| Meaning-focused output | ☑ | Developing fluency | ☐ |

WHAT IS IT?

Cognates are words that have similar forms and meanings across languages. A large number of Spanish–English cognates can be identified in English academic vocabulary because of their shared Latin roots. Bushong (2010) identified the presence of Spanish–English cognates on the AWL, and many of these same words can be found on the Middle School Vocabulary Lists. Bushong's complete list can be found at http://etd.fcla.edu/CF/CFE0003528/Bushong_Robert_W_201012_MA.pdf

WHY DO IT?

By assisting ELLs whose first language is Spanish to develop their aware-ness of cognates, and by teaching strategies for using cognates, teachers provide a powerful tool for developing word recognition and reading comprehension. This activity might also assist English speakers who are learning Spanish as a second language.

HOW TO IMPLEMENT

1. Select a passage from your course text and identify a short list of cognates in that passage.

2. Introduce cognates to students. Explain that they can use their knowledge of word meanings in Spanish to help them understand English words in their textbooks.

3. Write a cognate pair on the board. Have students think about what the word means in both languages.

4. Have students volunteer sentences using the target word in both languages.

5. Place students in pairs or small groups. Have students do the following:

   • Silently read the selected text passage.

   • Work together to identify words they think might have a Spanish cognate.

   • Use the meaning of the Spanish word and write a prediction of what the word means in English.

   • Confirm results by checking to see if the word's meaning makes sense in the passage.

6. Monitor groups' discussions. Provide feedback and additional explanation if needed.

7. Have students do the following:

   • Come back together as a class.

   • Volunteer to share their cognates and word meanings.

   • Listen to other groups' word meaning decisions.

8. Facilitate this discussion. Guide students to the appropriate contex-tual meanings of the words discussed.

FIX-UPS

• English and Spanish share true cognates, partial cognates, and false cognates. Begin with true cognates. When students become comfortable identifying true cognates, you can provide instruction in other categories.

• If you have difficulty identifying Spanish–English cognates, you can do the following:

   • Refer to Table 4.1.

- Refer to a Spanish–English dictionary.
- Refer to Bushong's (2010) lists of true, partial, and false Spanish–English cognates on the AWL.
- Perform an Internet search.
- Table 4.1 can assist students who have difficulty identifying English words with Spanish cognates.

Table 4.1.   Spanish–English cognate chart

Part of speech	Spanish syllable affected	To convert to English	Spanish forms (sample)	English forms (sample)
Nouns	Ending in -or	Very often no change	actor, color, favor	actor, color, favor
	Ending in -al	Very often no change	animal, capital, hospital	animal, capital, hospital
	Ending in -ista	Delete -a; may have spelling modifications	artista, dentista, novelista	artist, dentist, novelist
	Ending in -ismo	Delete -o; may have spelling modifications	idealismo, turismo, optimismo	idealism, tourism, optimism
	Ending in -ncia	Delete -ia; may have spelling modifications	asistencia, licencia, inteligencia	assistance, license, intelligence
	Ending in -dad	Delete -dad, add -ty; may have spelling modifications	variedad, sociedad, electricidad	variety, society, electricity
Adjectives	Ending in -ivo or -iva	Delete -ivo/-iva, add -ive; may have spelling modifications	negativo, positivo, expresivo	negative, positive, expressive
	Ending in -al	Very often no change	final, usual, normal	final, usual, normal
	Ending in -oso	Delete -oso, add -ous; may have spelling modifications	famoso, nervioso, delicioso	famous, nervous, delicious
	Ending in -ble	May have spelling modifications	horrible, imposible, terrible	horrible, impossible, terrible

(continued)

Table 4.1. *(continued)*

Part of speech	Spanish syllable affected	To convert to English	Spanish forms (sample)	English forms (sample)
	Ending in -nte	Delete final -e; may have spelling modifications	ignorante, conveniente, paciente	ignorant, convenient, patient
	Ending in -ido	Delete final -o	rapido, solido, valido	rapid, solid, valid
	Ending in -il	Add -e to the end	fertil, hostil, juvenil	fertile, hostile, juvenile
	Ending in -ario	Delete -ario, add -ary; may have spelling modifications	secundario, literario, ordinario	secondary, literary, ordinary
Verbs	Ending in -ar	Delete -ar, add -ate; may have spelling modifications	crear, calcular, concentrar	create, calculate, concentrate
	Infinitives ending in -ar, -er, or -ir	Delete -ar, -er, or -ir (in English infinitive verbs ending in vowel + consonant + t)	insultar, consultar, presentar	insult, consult, present
	Infinitives ending in -ar, -er, or -ir	Delete ending and add final -e (in English infinitive verbs ending in vowel + consonant + e)	acusar, aadorar, autorizar	accuse, adore, authorize
	Infinitives ending in -ificar	Delete ending and add final -y	unificar, simplificar, solidificar	unify, simplify, solidify
Adverbs	Final -mente on feminine adjectives to make adverbial form	Delete ending and add -ly	normalmente, naturalmente, finalmente	normally, naturally, finally

EXTENSIONS

Quick Writing

- Have students summarize what they have learned from the selected passage.
- Have students reflect on how recognizing cognates helped them understand the passage, using examples.

Word Sorts Have students sort word pairs that are true cognates, partial cognates, and false cognates.

Word Wall Add true Spanish–English cognate pairs to your classroom word wall.

Vocabulary Cards Have students add cognate information to their vocabulary cards.

WORD BUILDER

Meaning-focused input	☐	Language-focused learning	☑
Meaning-focused output	☑	Developing fluency	☐

WHAT IS IT?

Word building is a tactile activity in which students create new words by combining a base word with multiple prefixes and suffixes.

WHY DO IT?

Word building provides students opportunities to do the following:

- Use a hands-on approach to create new words.
- Analyze word parts and consider how they change the meaning and function of a base word.
- Reinforce their spelling skills.
- Support their grammatical knowledge.
- Develop their understanding of the meanings of target words and multiple affixes at the same time.

HOW TO IMPLEMENT

1. Choose a target academic base word relevant to the content you are teaching. Think about the possible prefixes and/or suffixes that can be combined with that word. Jot down potential new words that can be created by combining the base word with different affixes. You can refer to the Middle School Vocabulary Lists in Chapter 6, and for expanded options you can use an online dictionary.

2. Discuss the meaning of the base word with students. If the word has more than one meaning, focus on the meaning of the word in the text. Have students volunteer to name the word's part of speech.

3. Discuss the meanings of the selected prefixes and suffixes.

4. On a SMART Board or on a PowerPoint using an overhead projector, demonstrate building one or two words by manipulating the prefixes and suffixes and the base word. Talk through required spelling changes as you do this.

5. Model a sentence using the built word and have students tell you their ideas about the new word's meaning and function in the sentence.

6. Provide students with a sheet of paper and small sticky notes (if these are not readily available, small pieces of scrap paper will work as well).

7. Place students in pairs or small groups. Have students do the following:

   • Fold the sheet of paper into three sections horizontally.

   • Write the base form of the word on one note and selected prefixes and suffixes on additional notes; they should have one note for each selected prefix and suffix.

   • Place the base form of the word in the center section on their folded piece of paper; prefixes should be placed in the section to the left of the base word and suffixes to the right.

   • Build as many words as they can by attaching selected prefixes and suffixes to the base word; students record each word they make in the center section of their sheet of paper.

FIX-UPS

• Consider your students' developmental levels when determining how many prefixes and suffixes you will use in this activity. You may want to begin with only one or two suffixes and then add more options in a later lesson.

• Assist your students by explaining spelling conventions associated with various suffixes. As an example, the letter *a* needs to be added to the base word *interpret* before adding the suffix *-tion*.

EXTENSIONS

Quick Writing   Have students complete a quick write describing the process they used to build new words and what they learned in doing so.

Triple-Entry Journal   Have students make an entry in their triple-entry journals based on this activity.

WORD CHAINS FOR FORM, MEANING, AND USE

Meaning-focused input	☐	Language-focused learning	☑
Meaning-focused output	☐	Developing fluency	☐

WHAT IS IT?

The word chain strategy requires students to link related words by connecting their form, meaning, or use and to state the reason behind those connections (Rasinski, 2006).

WHY DO IT?

Incorporating word chain activities in your classroom will accomplish the following:

- Help students make meaningful connections between words.

- Require students to justify the meaning connections they have made between words.

- Allow students opportunities to discover relationships between a word's structure and its grammatical role.

- Allow students opportunities to discover relationships between a word's grammatical role and its meaning.

HOW TO IMPLEMENT WORD CHAINS FOR FORM AND USE

1. Choose a target word or words. Identify possible morphological variations. Example:

    Target word: *define*

    Morphological variations: definable, defined, defines, defining, definition, definitions

2. Plan a series of prompts to guide students as they change the word based on its form. These prompts can look something like this:

    - Take out a piece of paper and write the word *define* at the top. What does *define* mean? Is it a noun, verb, or adjective? Write your answer next to *define*.

    - Now, drop the -*e* and add -*able* to the end of the word. What is the new word? Is *definable* a noun, verb, or adjective? Write your answer next to *definable*.

    - Drop the -*able* and add -*ed*. What is the new word? Is *defined* a noun, verb, or adjective? Write your answer next to *defined*.

    - Drop the -*d* and add -*s*. What is the new word? Is *defines* a noun, verb, or adjective? Write your answer next to *defines*.

    - Drop the -*es* and add -*ing*. What is the new word? Is *defining* a noun, verb, or adjective? Write your answer next to *defining*.

    - Now, drop the -*ing* and add -*ition*. What is the new word? Is *definition* a noun, verb, or adjective? Write your answer next to *definition*.

    - Now, add an -*s* to the end of *definition*. What is the new word? Is *definitions* a noun, a verb, or adjective? Write your answer next to *definitions*.

3. Initiate a whole-class discussion about this activity. First, talk about the similarities in meaning between these words, then talk about how the changes in word endings alter the word meanings.

WORD CHAINS FOR MEANING

1. Select up to 10 academic words related to your current instructional topic. Example: *fraction, quotient, numerator, denominator, equivalent*

2. Have students chain these words by describing their meanings in relationship to the next word in their chain. It might look something like this:

   - A *quotient* is made by dividing one number by another.

   - A *fraction* is another way to express a quotient.

   - In a fraction, the *numerator* is divided by the *denominator*.

   - Fractions with different numerators and denominators that represent the same amount are *equivalent* fractions.

3. Initiate a whole-class discussion about this activity. Have groups volunteer to share their chains and their connections. Encourage conversation about the different connections groups might have made between terms.

FIX-UPS

- If students are new to word chaining for meaning, model the process for them first. Then have students work through the process in pairs or small groups before asking them to complete a chain independently.

- If students have difficulty with the process, you can make it easier by asking them to chain two words and then add additional words one at a time.

- You can select target words yourself, or you can let students select the words they would like to target.

- Alternately, you can provide students with a list of up to 20 words and allow them to develop chains using a subset of your list.

EXTENSIONS

Quick Writing   Have students do a quick write based upon this chaining activity.

4-3-2 for Fluency   Have students use word chains for meaning as preparation for their 4-3-2 for Fluency talks.

ACTIVITIES FOR DEVELOPING FLUENCY

The activities in this section will assist students in developing their abilities to incorporate new vocabulary with speed and accuracy in speaking and writing activities.

4-3-2 FOR FLUENCY

Meaning-focused input	☐	Language-focused learning	☐
Meaning-focused output	☑	Developing fluency	☑

WHAT IS IT?

A 4-3-2 for Fluency is a timed speaking activity that provides students opportunities to practice incorporating academic vocabulary in speaking to help them increase speed and accuracy when using new words (Arevart & Nation, 1991; Nation, 1989). The more students use new words in speaking, the more likely they are to use them in writing (Coxhead, 2008). Students prepare a 4-minute talk on a topic they are currently studying. They give their talk to a partner and then switch partners. Students give their talk again, this time in 3 minutes. This process is repeated a third time with a third partner and 2 minutes in which to give their talk.

WHY DO IT?

A 4-3-2 for Fluency provides students the opportunity to accomplish the following:

- Prepare a talk on a content-related topic they know well.

- Reinforce their understanding of the concepts they are speaking about.

- Develop their understanding of the meanings and use of the target academic words.

- Learn target academic and technical vocabulary through listening to other students' talks (meaning-focused input).

- Learn target academic and technical vocabulary through using it in speaking (meaning-focused output).

- Increase their fluency using target academic and technical vocabulary by repeating their talk multiple times in shorter increments of time.

- Develop confidence using academic and technical words in speech.

HOW TO IMPLEMENT

1. Introduce students to the idea of a 4-3-2 for Fluency. Explain why this is an important activity and the ways in which it will help them learn.

2. Choose a topic that is familiar to your students and target a reasonable number of academic words related to that topic. Write the topic and the words on the board or an overhead projector.

3. Have students brainstorm ideas that can be incorporated into a 4-minute talk. Make sure they are including target academic words in their ideas.

4. Model a talk using students' ideas. Include targeted academic words in your talk. Ask a student volunteer to time your talk to 4 minutes.

5. Place students in small groups. Have groups choose a current content-related topic and brainstorm ideas for a talk on that topic using targeted academic words. Each student in the group should be taking notes and preparing their individual talks based upon the group's discussion.

6. Have students find a partner who was not in their original group. Partners take turns giving their 4-minute talks to each other.

7. Have students find a second partner who was not in their original group. Partners take turns giving 3-minute talks to each other.

8. Have students find a third partner who was not in their original group. Partners take turns giving 2-minute talks to each other.

9. Listening partners should monitor their speaking partner's content and use of targeted academic words in talks.

10. Follow up with a whole-class discussion about the activity they just completed and what they have learned.

FIX-UPS

*   This activity is an excellent way to help students prepare for an upcoming quiz or test. If this is the case, you may want to select separate topics for each group.

*   Do not expect perfection! Remind students that this activity may feel awkward at first, but the more practice they have talking about what they have learned, the more confident they will become.

*   Keep your students' developmental levels in mind when planning this activity. You may find that 4 minutes is too long. If so, you can shorten the time increments for student talks.

*   You can assist your students' selection of partners by assigning a number to each group (i.e., groups 1, 2, 3, and 4). For the first round, all 1s partner with 4s and 2s partner with 3s. For the second round, all 1s partner with 3s and 2s partner with 4s. For the third round, all 1s partner with 2s and 3s partner with 4s.

*   Monitor group planning and provide additional feedback and modeling as needed.

EXTENSIONS

Quick Writing

*   Have students do a quick write based on the content they included in their 4-3-2 for Fluency talks.

*   Have students reflect on their experiences preparing for and giving their 4-3-2- for Fluency talks.

QUICK WRITING

Meaning-focused input	☐	Language-focused learning	☐
Meaning-focused output	☑	Developing fluency	☑

WHAT IS IT?

Quick writing (Tompkins, 2014) is a multipurpose strategy useful for helping students develop writing fluency. Students are provided a prompt and have a limited amount of time (2–10 minutes) to respond to the prompt. Quick writes may be used as a before-, during-, or after-reading activity. They also offer opportunities for informal assessments of student learning.

WHY DO IT?

Incorporating the quick write strategy in your classroom provides students opportunities to accomplish the following:

- Develop their use of academic vocabulary in writing fluency.
- Explore their background knowledge about a topic.
- Summarize a reading.
- Compare and contrast between ideas, make predictions, or hypothesize.
- Encourage critical thinking through evaluation of ideas.
- Generate new ideas.

HOW TO IMPLEMENT

1. Prepare a prompt for the quick write related to the content you are teaching. Encourage students' use of academic vocabulary by including it in your prompt. Examples:
   - Think about the word *democracy*. What does it mean? Who has power in a *democracy*?
   - Think about a person who has an *unhealthy lifestyle*. How does their *lifestyle affect* their friends, their families, and their community?
   - If I say that something is *logical*, what does that mean? Do you always agree with other people's *logic*?
   - Tell me what you know about *congruent* objects (remind students to incorporate words such as *dimension* and *equal*).
   - What is the difference between an *element* and a *compound*?

2. Tell students what a quick write is and how it will help their learning. Explain that in a quick write, they do not need to worry about spelling or grammar. They just need to quickly write about their ideas.

3. Model a quick write response on the board or an overhead projector. You can also model getting stuck and discuss different suggestions for getting unstuck with your students.

4. Have students do a quick write response to a different prompt. Tell them the amount of time they have to complete their quick write. Consider the requirements of the prompt when determining the time limit; generally, you should allow 10 minutes or less for a quick write.

FIX-UPS

- Students who are new to quick writing may require more guidance in their prompts. As students become more familiar with the process, you can gradually decrease the amount of information in the prompts.

- Depending on students' developmental levels, you may have them work in pairs or groups to complete a quick write.

- If students are stuck, scaffold them by providing additional modeling, asking for examples, reminding them about what they may already know about the topic, or further developing your prompt.

EXTENSIONS

Vocabulary Cards   Have students create vocabulary cards using the target words in their quick write.

4-3-2 for Fluency   Have students use their quick writes to prepare 4-3-2 for Fluency talks.

SUMMARY

In this chapter, we outlined 14 activities to assist students in learning both academic and technical words they will frequently encounter when reading their content-area textbooks. While teachers might have some familiarity with these activities, they have been adapted with a focus on developing students' knowledge of academic and technical vocabulary situated within the strands of meaning-focused input, meaning-focused output, language-focused learning, and fluency development.

It is of critical importance, however, that teachers do not spend instructional time focusing on words that their students already know. In Chapter 5, we discuss what it means to fully know a word and present assessments for determining the words students know now.

DISCUSSION QUESTIONS

1. Think about the different activities described in this chapter. For each strategy, ask yourself if it is new to you, or if you have

learned about it before. If you already know about this strategy, ask yourself how often you incorporate it in your vocabulary learning classroom. Why have you used it? Why not?

2. If you have learned a new activity idea in this chapter, what are its strengths and weaknesses for your classroom? What adaptations would you consider making to these activities, and why?

Knowing a Word and Testing Word Knowledge

5

ANTICIPATION ACTIVITY

1. What knowledge about words do learners need to read and write in English? Is that knowledge the same as the knowledge they need for speaking and listening?

2. What factors can affect the ease or difficulty of learning a word in English?

3. What do teachers need to think about when testing vocabulary knowledge?

WHAT DOES IT MEAN TO KNOW A WORD?

Have you ever tried to define the word *word*? It seems like a fairly simple concept—you can use an example such as *the words in a book*, but beyond that, what do you need to know in order to know the word *word*? If an emergent reader were learning concepts of print, that reader could identify a word by its representation as a series of marks within spaces (McKenna & Stahl, 2009, p. 76), but that definition focuses on the written word, and for this reason carries its own set of limitations. How could that definition be amended to include its spoken form? Is it that people can recognize *word* as it is pronounced in conversation or can pronounce *word* so that others can recognize it? Clearly, there is more to knowing *word* than simply being able to recognize or produce *word* in speaking and writing—its meaning(s) must be known when it is recognized and, in order to use it appropriately in communication, its function must be understood.

What Is Included in Knowing the Form of a Word?

Continue to consider the word *word*. What do people need to know in order recognize it and produce it orally? First, they need some phonemic knowledge—the understanding that words consist of specific phonemes (units of speech sounds). *Word* has three phonemes [wṛd], so speakers would need the ability to produce and recognize the two consonants and the *r*-controlled vowel in *word* as a unit within a stream of speech. In addition, we need to consider word stress in pronunciation. *Word* itself has only one syllable, so that makes it relatively easy to pronounce. Keep in mind, though, that English is a stress-timed language, which means that in multisyllable words, one syllable carries more stress than others. The family members of *word* (e.g., *worded, wordy, wordiness, wording*) have more than one syllable, so you would need to know English stress patterns in order to pronounce these forms of *word* correctly. This is intuitive for English speakers; however, ELLs need to learn word stress patterns in English to assist listening comprehension and spoken production.

Reading and writing requires a bit more work. *Word* can be identified in text by its orthographic form (i.e., it has four letters and a distinct spelling). To recognize it when reading it, readers need graphophonic knowledge (letter–sound correspondence) to assist in decoding the consonants and the *r*-controlled vowel in *word* and to spell it correctly.

What Is Included in Knowing the Function of a Word?

In addition to simply recognizing and producing the spoken and written forms of *word,* it is also important to know something about its grammatical roles and morphological variations, and these can be difficult to separate because one affects the other. Here is an example: *word* is a noun, and when morpheme *-s* is added (*words*), it makes a plural noun. However, when the morpheme *-ed* is added to *word* (i.e., it was *worded* incorrectly), then *word* changes to a verb. What if *-y* is added to *word* (*wordy*)? Now it becomes an adjective, as in "My goodness, this vocabulary book is *wordy!*" For more fun, change that *-y* to *-i* and add *-ness*, and now it becomes *wordiness*, which makes *word* a noun again. It is clear that these grammatical and morphological variations contribute to the meaning of *word* in communication (for more in-depth discussion of these ideas, see Nation, 2013; Schmitt, 2000).

What Is Included in Knowing the Meaning of a Word?

Let us go back to the question, "Have you ever tried to define the word *word*?" and try to come up with a good definition that focuses solely on meaning. A quick look-up on Dictionary.com gives several meanings of *word*. It could be said that a *word* is a principal carrier of meaning. *Words* can refer to a quarrel, as in "She was mad and we had *words*." The phrase "a word" can refer to a short talk, as in "I'd like to have *a word* with you." *Word* can also refer to a promise, as in "He gave his word." These examples illustrate the idea that English words often carry more than one meaning, so to fully know the meaning of a word, English speakers are required to know those multiple meanings. To complicate matters further, many words in English come from different origins, so they may have the same form but they carry completely different meanings. These words are referred to as *homonyms,* and they can be subdivided into two categories. First there are words like *to, too,* and *two; your* and *you're; its* and *it's*, which sound exactly the same yet have completely different spellings and meanings. These words are called *homophones.* English speakers often have difficulties using homophones correctly in written form, so it is not surprising that ELLs can find their uses confusing to sort out. *Homographs* are the second category, and these are words that have the identical written form and different meanings (e.g., *bark* like a dog, the *bark* on a tree).

What Must Be Known in Order to Use a Word Correctly?

Teachers often encounter situations in which students try to incorporate new vocabulary in their written work and use a word with the right meaning, but not in the way the word is commonly used.

Nation (2013) explains that there are three different layers of knowledge that come into play when people make word choices. The first is knowledge of grammatical patterning (i.e., the patterns in which words can be used in sentences). As an example, the verbs *brought* and *fetched* can be used in sentences containing an indirect object, but the verbs *carried* and *transported* cannot:

The dog *brought* me a bone.

The dog *fetched* me a bone.

The dog *carried* me a bone.

The dog *transported* me a bone.

The second layer of knowledge needed in word choice is collocational knowledge. Certain words are used frequently with other words in chunks of language that are used over and over again, and these chunks are referred to as *collocations.* As an example, English speakers may say "in his old age" but do not say "in his young age"; instead, they would say something like "in his youth." In this example, *age* collocates frequently with *old,* but not with *young.*

Here is another example. To express devotion to another, one could say, "I love you so much" or "I love you very much," but if one says, "I love you too much," it results in an entirely different meaning. The words *so, very,* and *too* are all collocates of *much,* and each is an intensifier in these sentences, so it would be logical to think that they would all intensify the amount of love being expressed. However, it is clear that in the third sentence, the phrase *too much* has an almost apologetic stance to it. Beyond grammatical and collocational knowledge, Nation points out that appropriateness of word choice must also be understood. Knowledge of frequency plays an important role in making these choices.

To truly understand the word *word,* the ways in which it is used must be considered. Certainly, *word* is a high-frequency word (especially in this book!). It is used regularly, both in its spoken and written forms. That said, *word* has synonyms (e.g., *utterance, statement, expression, declaration, remark*). So what if a student replaced *word* with *utterance,* as in the sentence "He answered the question with one *utterance*"? *Utterance* is not wrong, exactly, in this sentence, but it is not exactly right, either. Frequency of word use is a good reason why this sentence is a bit off and why *word* might be preferred in the sentence.

Knowledge of *register,* which is the understanding that specific language might be appropriate for one social or occupational setting, but not for another (Wardhaugh, 2002), also plays a role in making good word choices. There are formal registers and less formal ones, and it is important that students know this distinction. Consider the synonyms for *word* in the previous paragraph; which of these would be used in different registers? *Utterance* and *remark* seem more formal. *Statement* is formal as well, but it would more likely be used in political or legal contexts, as in "The congressman issued a statement to the reporters" or "He gave his statement to the police."

Slang is a great example of an informal register. There are some excellent current slangy uses of *word*; here are a few: "Word-up!" (here, *word* is used as a greeting), "What's the word?" (i.e., "What's going on?"), or, our personal favorite, "Word!" meaning, "I hear you" or "I've got it." People also use [first initial] + *word* as a euphemism for words they do not actually want to say. As an example, many people would not use a profane word in a formal setting (or at all!), but refer to it as "the *f*-word" instead. Or, if there were a topic some people were trying to avoid, such as marriage, they might refer to it as "the *m*-word."

To continue teasing out the meaning of *word,* Marzano (2004) described a word as a "packet of knowledge" (p. 32). In other words, the word *word* refers to everything people already know about words; all of their experiences with words are neatly organized into a packet of information with a label on it, which is *word*. This includes multiple meanings, possible homographs and homophones, synonyms, spelling, pronunciation, phonological and grammatical knowledge, and an understanding of word frequency and register.

WHAT MAKES WORD LEARNING EASY AND WHAT MAKES IT DIFFICULT?

This section explores ideas about word learning from three well-known vocabulary researchers. Michael Graves (2006) examined the different types of tasks that students are required to do when learning new words, Beck et al. (2002) explained the word-learning process in terms of a continuum ranging from not knowing a word at all to having a decontextualized understanding of its meaning and the ability to use it metaphorically, and Paul Nation (1990, 2013) described the learning burden involved in learning new words. These are separate yet interrelated topics, so we will break them down and build connections between them, giving examples to assist in contextualizing them.

Graves (2006) identified seven distinct tasks that word learners must complete, and some of these tasks are easier than others. From infancy, typically developing children have the ability to hear and produce any sound in any given language, and they begin learning the language(s) surrounding them right away. The first task for children is to develop a basic oral vocabulary, and generally the words they learn are those that will help them fulfill their needs. Whether a child is learning English or a different home language, they can still be expected to develop a basic oral vocabulary. ELLs are expected to develop a second basic oral vocabulary when they enter school; for those students, this task is made somewhat easier because they already know the concepts for many of the new words they are learning and they can map those words onto the concepts they already have.

The second task students face is learning to read words they already know, and although this task is often far easier said than done, it is all a part of the vocabulary-learning process, because part of knowing a word is the ability to recognize its written form. ELLs in the early grades are expected to develop a basic oral vocabulary in English and read its written form at the same time, which produces additional challenges for them.

Although learning a language and learning to read it at the same time is a difficult process, teachers can reduce the learning burden of words (Nation, 1990, 2013) by considering a few basic questions related to the word's form, its meaning, and its function in English, and planning instructional events based on this evaluation. For example, is the target word frequently used? In other words, is the student likely to have multiple encounters with the word through conversation? Also, how familiar are the sounds and the stress pattern of the target word? This can either increase or decrease the learning burden for ELLs, because some English phonemes do not exist in other languages (e.g., /z/ does not exist in Spanish). In addition, if a student's home language is not stress-timed, as English is, there may be difficulty with pronouncing and recognizing word stress in English words.

Children raised in English-speaking homes also encounter words they have never seen or heard before and about which they have no knowledge. When this happens, Beck and colleagues (2002) would place these students at the earliest stage of the word-learning continuum, which is having no knowledge of the word at all. These could be low-frequency words they encounter during reading or hear in conversation. Graves (2006) made a point that, even if a child has never seen or heard a word before, he or she may still have a concept for that word. As an example, a student may hear the word *marveled* and have no idea what it means. However, they may know the feeling of being amazed by something, and once that connection is established, it provides a shortcut for learning the meaning of *marveled*. At the same time, the student may be able to understand that to marvel at something is a good thing, based upon the context in which he or she hears the word. In this case, the child is in the second stage of the word-learning continuum described by Beck and colleagues (2002).

When considering the learning burden for words like this, Nation (1990, 2013) recommended that the teacher consider whether a student could make contextual predictions for word meaning, or whether the meaning could be predicted by the word's form (i.e., identifying base words and affixes). Helping students develop strategies to assist them in these areas can help reduce the learning burden of these words.

Think back to your days in middle school. Most likely you encountered many new words that represented concepts that were also entirely new to you. Learning these words and concepts together is another task described by Graves (2006). On Beck and colleagues' (2002) continuum of word learning, these types of words, when learned, would fall into the category of words that are context-bound. Beck and colleagues used the following example: *a radiant bride*. In this case, a radiant bride could be a bride who glows with happiness. A student may have heard the words *radiant* and *bride* together many times and have gleaned some understanding that a radiant bride exhibits the characteristics of happiness; however, even if the student understands that concept, it would be difficult to generalize it to *radiant heat* in science class.

The next two tasks Graves (2006) described for word learners have to do with building understanding of known words. Here a student may need to learn a new meaning for a word he or she knows, or may be developing understanding of the multiple uses of that word. In the example of *radiant bride* and *radiant heat*, gaining the ability to understand words in both contexts is a good representation of this task.

To reduce the learning burden of this task for word learners, teachers can ask themselves if the word meanings are related in some way (Nation, 1990, 2013). In the earlier example, the word *radiant* refers to glowing or giving off (something). In the case of a bride, she is glowing with happiness, which is fairly abstract; however, radiant heat refers to something that is already hot and gives off that heat, so these meanings are related in some way, and teachers can assist students in making connections between these meanings when learning new words.

The final task Graves (2006) had for a word learner is the ability to use new words in speaking and writing. On the Beck and colleagues (2002) continuum for learning new words, one of the final stages described is the phenomenon of a word being on the tip of the tongue; that is, a person knows he or she knows the word, knows it would be the exact right word for the purpose, but is unable to remember it and produce it. Such a person has not achieved fluency in using this word (Nation, 2007); such fluency comes at the final stage when the person is not only able to use the word, but also has a strong enough understanding of its various forms, meanings, and uses to apply it metaphorically (Beck et al., 2002).

Clearly, there is quite a lot to know in order to truly know a word. Fortunately, people do not need to know all words at this level. That being said, middle school students who are expected to independently read and learn and respond to texts containing academic vocabulary under the rigors of the CCSS will need support to assist them in gaining control of that vocabulary's form, meaning, and function.

DETERMINING HOW MANY WORDS FROM THE MIDDLE SCHOOL VOCABULARY LISTS STUDENTS ALREADY KNOW

Vocabulary knowledge is incremental in nature (Schmitt, 2010). As can be seen from the previous discussion about what it means to know a word, various aspects of word knowledge can be added to students' *receptive* (recognizing words contextually in reading or listening and figuring out their meanings) and *productive* (appropriately using words in speaking or writing) abilities. However, how do teachers assess where students are in building vocabulary knowledge? This is an important question because teachers do not want to waste classroom time focusing on words or aspects of words their students already know.

One very simple way to find out which words students know from a particular content area of the Middle School Vocabulary Lists is to use a yes/no test in which students work down the list and indicate, with a check or a cross-out, which words they know the meaning of and which ones they do not. To increase understanding of how much students know, or what they might want to know about specific words, teachers can ask students to indicate how easily they think they can use the words in speaking or writing. Another method is to ask students to indicate what they would like to learn about particular words. Teachers can use the results of these simple tests to guide planning.

TESTING STUDENTS' LEARNING OF MIDDLE SCHOOL VOCABULARY LIST WORDS

Part of planning for vocabulary is thinking about how to measure students' learning. A low-key approach is to have a regular assessment on the words students have worked on in class over recent weeks. Testing word learning needs to take into account both students' receptive and productive capabilities using new words, as well as their understanding of words' forms, meanings, and usage patterns. For example, teachers could ask students to decide which aspects of words they would like to be assessed on, such as spelling, meaning, common collocations, and so on. Students might also be asked to use the target words in speaking or writing tasks.

In this section we have described how teachers can determine which words from the Middle School Vocabulary List students might already know. Once this is done, teachers will know which words to focus students' attention on. From there, it is important to regularly assess students' increasing knowledge of these words, and some suggestions have been made in this area.

Teachers might have questions about how many words their students, or a specific student, might know. The next section discusses how vocabulary size testing can be done.

DETERMINING HOW MANY WORDS STUDENTS KNOW

It is important to find out how many words students know as part of the benchmarking for any curriculum-based vocabulary program. Estimates of students' vocabulary size are useful as indicators of whether certain vocabulary is likely already known, which assists in planning. Further, once teachers understand students' vocabulary size, it is far easier to match that student with a text the student can read and understand.

Nation and Coxhead (2014) tested the vocabulary sizes of students (ages 13–18) in secondary schools in New Zealand. Early findings suggest that for average native speakers of English, a basic guideline can be used when it comes to vocabulary size. Take the age of the young native English speaker, subtract 2 or 3 years from that number, and multiply that by 1,000. That means that a 15-year-old native English speaker is likely to have a vocabulary size of around 13,000 words (15 − 2 x 1,000 = 13,000). Actual vocabulary size may vary substantially, however, because some 15-year-olds might be voracious readers, for instance, or online gamers (who appear to have larger vocabulary sizes than others their age), whereas others might not be so oriented to text or language.

Nonnative speakers of English are less likely to have a good match between the size of their vocabulary and the vocabulary size needed for school, particularly if the students do not live in an English-speaking country, have not been living in an English-speaking country for very long, or if they are not literate in their first language. In addition to studying native speaker vocabulary sizes in New Zealand secondary schools, Nation and Coxhead (2014) also studied the vocabulary sizes of nonnative English speakers (unreported data). These students' vocabulary sizes ranged from 5,600 word families to 14,800 word families. In the lower scoring set of data, one student was a 13-year-old from Pakistan and the other was a 14-year-old from China. Both students had been in New Zealand for 1 year or less. In contrast, a 15-year-old student from the Philippines who had been in New Zealand since age 11 (approximately 4 years) scored at the high end of the data. This learner's profile is much more like that of a native English speaker of the same age. These examples indicate the possible ranges in vocabulary size that our students might have, depending on their time in an English-speaking country and their age of arrival.

Students learning English as a foreign language have varying vocabulary sizes as well. As an example, an early study of Indonesian learners by Nurweni and Read (1999) found that after several years of studying English at the university level, the learners had an English vocabulary size of roughly 2,000 word families.

It is clear that a student with a vocabulary of roughly 5,000 word families will need more support to read texts that have a vocabulary load of 8,000–9,000 word families than a student who has a vocabulary size of 14,000 word families. For teachers of struggling readers, assessing students' vocabulary size can help to isolate the students' difficulties. If a struggling reader has a small vocabulary, it is reasonable to expect that a focus on vocabulary development could be the key. On the other hand, a struggling reader with a large vocabulary likely has difficulties outside of vocabulary knowledge, and other efforts can be directed toward reading support.

The Vocabulary Size Test

Nation's Vocabulary Size Test (VST; Coxhead, Nation, & Sim, in press; Nation & Beglar, 2007; Nation & Coxhead, 2014) can be used to find out the overall number of words your students know in English. Figure 5.1 is an example of an item from the VST. The target word is given in a sentence and the test taker chooses the correct meaning from a list of choices. The drawbacks of multiple-choice tests are well known, including problems such as not being able to guarantee the learner's answer is not based in guessing. Nation and Coxhead's (2014) testing project in New Zealand showed that test takers who took two versions of the test scored roughly the same score each time.

16. **strap** He broke the *strap*.

    a   promise

    b   top cover

    c   shallow dish for food

    d   strip of strong material

Figure 5.1. Example of an item from the Vocabulary Size Test. (From Nation, I.S.P. [n.d.-b]. *Vocabulary size test version A*. Retrieved from http://www.victoria.ac.nz/lals/about/staff/publications/paul-nation/VST-version-A.pdf; reprinted by permission.)

The VST is a receptive vocabulary test, which means that it tests word and meaning recognition, rather than testing whether learners can use or produce a word. The VST comes in two versions: one that tests up to the 14,000-word level and one that tests up to the 20,000-word level. It begins with high-frequency vocabulary at the first 1,000 words and goes in 1,000-word bands up to 14,000 or 20,000 words (depending upon the version). Table 5.1 shows some examples of words at the 1,000, 5,000, 10,000, 15,000, and 20,000 frequency levels. The 14,000-word-level version would be a good choice for a student at the middle school level. This test can be taken and automatically scored on the Compleat Lexical Tutor web site by Tom Cobb (http://www.lextutor.ca/tests/levels/recognition/1_14k/; n.d.).

Adults have larger vocabularies than younger people in general, so teachers who wish to test their own vocabulary should take the 20,000-word-level version of the VST. Two versions of the 20,000-level VST are available on Paul Nation's web site (http://www.victoria.ac.nz/lals/about/staff/paul-nation). It takes 20–40 minutes to take the test. Additionally, you can take both the 14,000-word and the 20,000-word versions of the VST on Myq Larsen's web site (http://my.vocabularysize.com), which will also score the test and provide you with the vocabulary size result. It is suggested that students take the test at the start of an academic year and not repeat the test for several years. This suggestion is due to the incremental nature of vocabulary learning; vocabulary does not necessarily grow larger by many words at a time, but it might increase in terms of the depth

Table 5.1. Examples of words on Nation's Vocabulary Size Test according to frequency level

1,000	5,000	10,000	15,000	20,000
bank	bail	tawny	paracetamol	debouch
doctor	horrified	upkeep	caudal	factitious
he	staircase	lubricant	troposphere	gerontocracy
simple	grunt	chug	cyan	ingle

Source: Nation (n.d.-a).

of knowledge of learning more about different aspects of words. It is also important that learners take all the levels of the test (see Nguyen & Nation, 2011, for a discussion of this point). The test is not a test of each level of 1,000 words; instead, the test taker's total score is taken as a sum. The score of the test is multiplied by 200 to get the vocabulary size total: for a student who took the test and scored 84/100, 84 is multiplied by 200, yielding a score of 16,800 words. (For more information about the development of the VST, see Nation & Beglar [2007] and Nation & Coxhead [2014].)

Teachers can also find bilingual versions of the VST for a range of languages on Paul Nation's web site (http://www.victoria.ac.nz/lals/about/staff/paul-nation; e.g., Vietnamese [Nguyen & Nation, 2011], Russian [Elgort, 2013], Mandarin, Spanish). Bilingual versions mean that learners have support from the knowledge of their first language when taking the test. For lower-level ELLs, that support might be particularly helpful. There are also specialized tests for learners who do not have much vocabulary in English, which are described in the following subsections.

The Vocabulary Levels Test

The Vocabulary Levels Test (Nation, 1990; Schmitt, Schmitt, & Clapham, 2001) takes another approach to testing receptive vocabulary knowledge. It tests learners at different vocabulary levels using different word lists, in this case the first and second 1,000-word families, then 3,000, 5,000, the AWL, and the 10,000-word family level. The scores in each section of the test are not added together as a total, but the scores at each level estimate the amount of vocabulary on that word list a student knows. Each section of the test has 30 items. If a student scores over 50% in a section, this result suggests that this person knows roughly half the items in the corresponding list. A score of over 20 items suggests that the student knows two-thirds of the items on the list. It is important that teachers share the results of the tests with learners so that they can set future vocabulary learning goals together based on the results.

Testing Vocabulary for Low-Level Learners or Those Who Cannot Read in English

For a student who is not able to read in English, a test consisting of written words would not be helpful in understanding how many words the student knows. Paul Nation has developed a series of picture tests for learners who do not have much vocabulary knowledge in English. The First 1,000 Words of English Test, for example, focuses on the first 1,000 words in English (Nation, 1993) and is available on Tom Cobb's Compleat Lexical Tutor web site (http://www.lextutor.ca/tests/levels/recognition/1k/test_1.html; it is titled the Levels 1k test). This test uses pictures and text, asking students to say whether they know a word, do not know it, or are not sure.

The Peabody Picture Test 4 (Dunn, Dunn, & Dunn, 2006) is not a vocabulary size test; however, it measures students' receptive vocabularies by comparing results to age- and grade-level norms. The test provides students with a target word and four pictures. Students point to the picture that matches the target word. This test contains 175 core vocabulary items.

The Expressive Vocabulary Test 2 (Williams, 2006) measures students' expressive (or productive) vocabulary knowledge. Like the Peabody Picture Test, the Expressive Vocabulary Test uses pictures. The examiner points to a picture and asks the student to say the word the picture represents. Student results are compared to age- and grade-level norms. When used in conjunction with the Peabody Picture Test, teachers are provided a clear understanding of the differences between a student's receptive and productive vocabulary knowledge. These are individualized assessments, however, and testing time for each is about 20 minutes, which makes them difficult to use for an entire class.

In this section we discussed a range of approaches for testing students' vocabulary knowledge. Next we examine how this might be useful for teaching and learning.

WHY IS THIS INFORMATION ABOUT VOCABULARY KNOWLEDGE AND TESTING IMPORTANT FOR MIDDLE SCHOOL TEACHERS AND LEARNERS?

One of the main purposes for assessing learning is to inform planning and teaching. The first thing for teachers to do is have students take the VST and talk about their results together. Different levels of vocabulary knowledge require different strategies. For learners who score around 3,000 or less on the VST, for example, the teacher can suggest that they focus on graded readers for independent study that are suitable for their vocabulary size. In the classroom, it would be important to actively and deliberately teach high-frequency words for this learner. The high-frequency words in English (and in any language) are vital as a building block for all language learning; they return the effort every day in all speaking, reading, writing, and listening activities. The words on the Middle School Vocabulary Lists are helpful for learners who need to grow their vocabulary up to 9,000 word families. The ultimate aim would be free reading of grade-level materials for study, which means a vocabulary of more than 9,000 word families for middle school students.

FUTURE RESEARCH AND CONSIDERATIONS

A student can fully know all of the words on the GSL and all of the words from the Middle School Science Vocabulary List and still have difficulties reading their course texts. As noted in the introduction to this book, students need to recognize about 98% of the words in a given text to read independently (Gillett, Temple, & Crawford, 2004), so, although knowing the words on the Middle School Vocabulary Lists will be tremendously beneficial to students, it will not necessarily be enough to enable them to read their textbooks independently. Students will still need to learn to use context clues to assist their recognition of low-frequency words.

Future research into middle school vocabulary could involve investigating multiword units in the corpus. For example, this research could look at common word patterns of the most frequent items in the mathematics corpus to find out more about how these words behave in the company of other words. Another avenue for research would be to find out more about this vocabulary in use by teachers and students at different age levels, in a variety of subjects, and in different contexts. We could look to see how learners develop their knowledge of this vocabulary. Finally, we could build on this research in wider contexts to see how this vocabulary from middle school textbooks is used internationally in textbooks in different contexts for learners of similar ages.

SUMMARY

In this chapter, we described the many different levels of knowledge necessary for fully knowing a word. We discussed what makes learning new words easy and what might make them more difficult to know. From there, we presented different methods for testing students' expressive and receptive vocabulary sizes, including tests for students who are unable to read or write in English. Finally, we presented some ideas for future research in this area, as well as some considerations for using the Middle School Vocabulary Lists in the classroom. The Middle School Vocabulary Lists can be found in Appendix A in this book.

CONCLUSION

In the introduction to this book, we stated three distinct purposes for writing it. The first purpose was to share the Middle School Vocabulary Lists with readers. The second purpose was to help readers understand the different kinds of vocabulary contained in content-area textbooks written for middle school students, and the third was to share some ideas for focusing students' attention on the academic and technical words they will encounter reading their course texts.

The first big idea readers should take away from this text is that there is a very specific academic and technical vocabulary that middle school students need to know; these words are important because they occur frequently in academic course texts. However, students will not often encounter these words outside their academic activities, so it is critical that teachers focus their attention on these words during instructional events.

The second big idea is that teachers can take a flexible approach when helping students focus on these words. Students can develop their understandings of these words through reading, writing, speaking, and listening activities as long as teachers incorporate emphasis on these words throughout these activities.

Finally, teachers should not be afraid to spend instructional time focusing students' attention on academic and technical vocabulary. The benefits are threefold: First, students will learn content at the same time they are learning academic and technical words. Second, students who have good control of the academic and technical words most frequently used in their content-area classrooms will be far better prepared for the rigors of instruction throughout their high school and university-level studies. Finally, and most important, a common goal for students is to help them prepare to be productive adults. Helping students develop understandings of words used in informational texts is an important step in meeting this goal.

DISCUSSION QUESTIONS

1.   Think back about what knowledge about a word is needed in order to know the word. How often do you come across words that you do not know in your reading? What are your strategies for learning that word, and what aspects of word knowledge do you focus on in that instance?

2.   In your classroom, what aspects of word knowledge do you address in class and what techniques do you use? Are there any aspects that you think need more of a focus in class? What are they, and what might you do to focus on them?

3.   Take the VST online, either on Tom Cobb's Compleat Lexical Tutor web site or Myq Larsen's my.vocabularysize.com. Think about the nature of the test and your learners. Would your learners need one-on-one support to take the test, or would they be capable of taking it in a small group? What benefits might there be for learners taking the test with a teacher alongside them?

4.   Using the Compleat Lexical Tutor web site, investigate the various vocabulary tests available, and think about the advantages and disadvantages of each one, keeping in mind a group of learners you are familiar with.

References

Alvermann, D.E., Phelps, S.F., & Gillis, V.R. (2010). *Content area reading and literacy* (6th ed.). Boston, MA: Allyn and Bacon.

Anders, P.L., & Bos, C.S. (1986). Semantic feature analysis: An interactive strategy for vocabulary development and text comprehension. *Journal of Reading, 29,* 610–616.

Arevart, S., & Nation, I.S.P. (1991). Fluency improvement in a second language. *RELC Journal, 22,* 84–94.

Bauer, L., & Nation, I.S.P. (1993). Word families. *International Journal of Lexicography, 6*(4), 253–279.

Baumann, F.J., Kame'enui, E.J., & Ash, G.W. (2003). Research on vocabulary instruction: Voltaire redux. In J. Flood, D. Lapp, J. Squire, & J. Jenson (Eds.), *Handbook of research on teaching the English language arts* (2nd ed., pp. 752–785). Mahwah, NJ: Erlbaum.

Beck, I.L., McKeown, M.G., & Kucan, L. (2002). *Bringing words to life: Robust vocabulary instruction.* New York, NY: Guilford Press.

Becker, W.C., Dixon, R., & Anderson-Inman, L. (1980). *Morphographic and root word analysis of 26,000 high frequency words.* Eugene: University of Oregon College of Education.

Berthoff, A.E. (1981). A curious triangle and the double-entry notebook: Or, how theory can help us teach reading and writing. In A. Berthoff (Ed.), *The making of meaning: Metaphors, models, and maxims for writing teachers* (pp. 30–47). Montclair, NJ: Boynton/Cook.

Biemiller, A. (2010). *Words worth teaching: Closing the vocabulary gap.* Columbus, OH: McGraw-Hill.

Blachowicz, C., & Fisher, P. (2000). Vocabulary instruction. In M. Kamil, P. Mosenthal, P.D. Pearson, & R. Barr (Eds.), *Handbook of reading research* (Vol. 3, pp. 503–523). Mahwah, NJ: Erlbaum.

Brezina, V., & Gablasova, D. (2013). Is there a core general vocabulary? Introducing the New General Service List. *Applied Linguistics.* Advance online publication. doi:10.1093/applin/amt018.

Bushong, R. (2010). *The Academic Word List reorganized for Spanish-speaking English language learners* (Unpublished master's thesis). University of Central Florida, Orlando. Retrieved from http://etd.fcla.edu/CF/CFE0003528/Bushong_Robert_W_201012_MA.pdf

Bushong, R., & Folse, K. (2012, March). *The Academic Word List reorganized for Spanish-speaking English language learners.* Paper presented at the meeting of TESOL, Philadelphia, PA.

Cobb, T. (n.d.). Compleat Lexical Tutor. Available at http://www.lextutor.ca

Coxhead, A. (2000). A new academic word list. *TESOL Quarterly, 34*(2), 213–238.

Coxhead, A. (2006). *Essentials of teaching academic vocabulary.* Boston, MA: Thomson Heinle.

Coxhead, A. (2008). *Using vocabulary in writing from input texts* (Unpublished doctoral dissertation). School of Linguistics and Applied Language Studies, Victoria University of Wellington, New Zealand.

Coxhead, A. (2012). Researching vocabulary in secondary school texts: *The Hunger Games* and more. *English in Aotearoa, 78,* 34–41.

Coxhead, A., Nation, P., & Sim, D. (in press). Creating and trialing six forms of the Vocabulary Size Test. *TESOLANZ Journal.*

Coxhead, A., Stevens, L., & Tinkle, J. (2010). Why might secondary science textbooks be difficult to read? *New Zealand Studies in Applied Linguistics, 16*(2), 37–52.

Cummins, J. (1979). Cognitive-academic language proficiency, linguistic interdependence, optimal age, and some other matters. *Working Papers in Bilingualism, 19,* 197–205.

Cummins, J. (Ed.). (1980). *The construct of language proficiency in bilingual education.* Washington, DC: Georgetown University Press.

Dale, E., & O'Rourke, J. (1981). *The living word vocabulary.* Chicago, IL: World Book-Childcraft International.

Davies, M. (2012). *Corpus of contemporary American English.* Available at http://corpus.byu.edu/coca

Davies, M., & Gardner, D. (2013). A new academic vocabulary list. *Applied Linguistics.* Advance online publication. doi:10.1093/applin/amt015.

Dolch, E.W. (1948). *Problems in reading.* Champaign, IL: Garrard Press.

Dunn, D.M., Dunn, L.W., & Dunn, L.M. (2006). *Peabody Picture Vocabulary Test–Fourth Edition (PPVT-4).* Bloomington, MN: American Guidance Service/Pearson.

Elgort, I. (2013). Effects of L1 definitions and cognate status on the Vocabulary Size Test of English as a foreign language. *Language Testing 30*(2), 253–272. Advance online publication. doi:10.1177/0265532212459028.

Erten, I.H., & Razi, S. (2009). The effects of cultural familiarity on reading comprehension. *Reading in a Foreign Language, 21,* 60–77.

Frayer, D.A., Frederick, W.C., & Klausmeier, H.J. (1969). A schema for testing the level of concept mastery. *Working Paper no. 16.* Madison: Wisconsin R&D Center for Cognitive Learning.

Fry, E.B., & Kress, J.E. (2006). *The reading teacher's book of lists: Grades K–12* (5th ed.). San Francisco, CA: Jossey Bass.

Gillett, J.W., Temple, C., & Crawford, A.N. (2004). *Understanding reading problems: Assessment and instruction* (6th ed.). Boston, MA: Allyn and Bacon.

Goulden, R., Nation, P., & Read, J. (1990). How large can a receptive vocabulary be? *Applied Linguistics, 11,* 341–363.

Gove, P.B. (Ed.). (1963). *Webster's third new international dictionary of the English language.* Springfield, MA: Merriam-Webster.

Graves, M. (2006). *The vocabulary book: Learning and instruction.* New York, NY: Teachers College Press.

Greene, J. (2008). *Academic vocabulary and formulaic language in middle school content area textbooks* (Unpublished doctoral dissertation). Georgia State University, Atlanta.

Guthrie, J.T., & Wigfield, A. (2000). Engagement and motivation in reading. In M.L. Kamil, P.B. Mosenthal, P.D. Pearson, & R. Barr (Eds.), *Handbook of reading research* (Vol. 3, pp. 403–422). New York, NY: Erlbaum.

Harris, A.J., & Jacobson, M.D. (1972). *Basic elementary reading vocabularies.* London, United Kingdom: Collier-Macmillan.

Heatley, A., Nation, P., & Coxhead, A. (2002). Range [Computer software]. Retrieved from http://www.victoria.ac.nz/lals/about/staff/paul-nation

Holt, Rinehart, and Winston. (2005). *Decisions for health: Level blue* (Texas ed.). Austin, TX: Author.

Hunston, S. (2002). *Corpora in applied linguistics.* Cambridge, United Kingdom: Cambridge University Press.

Hyland, K., & Tse, P. (2007). Is there an "academic vocabulary"? *TESOL Quarterly, 41*(2), 235–253.

Johnson, D., & Pearson, P.D. (1984). *Teaching reading vocabulary* (2nd ed.). New York, NY: Holt, Rinehart and Winston.

Kapinus, B., Pimental, S., & Dean, J. (2012, October 25). *Common core state standards for ELA/literacy* [Webinar]. Smarter Balanced Assessment Consortium.

Kobeleva, P.P. (2008). *The impact of unfamiliar proper names on ESL learners' listening comprehension* (Unpublished doctoral dissertation). Victoria University of Wellington, New Zealand.

Larsen, M. (n.d.). VocabularySize.com. Available at http://my.vocabularysize.com

Larson, R., Boswell, L., Kanold, T., & Stiff, L. (2007). *McDougal Littell math: Course 3* (Texas ed.). Evanston, IL: McDougal Littell.

Lowry, L. (1993). *The giver.* New York, NY: Random House.

Martinez, I.A., Beck, S.C., & Panza, C.B. (2009). Academic vocabulary in agriculture research articles: A corpus-based study. *English for Specific Purposes, 28,* 183–198.

Marzano, R. (2002). *Identifying the primary instructional concepts in mathematics: A linguistic approach.* Englewood, CO: Marzano and Associates.

Marzano, R. (2004). *Building background knowledge for academic achievement: Research on what works in schools.* Alexandria, VA: Association for Supervision and Curriculum Development.

Marzano, R.J., Kendall, J.S., & Paynter, D.E. (2005). A list of essential words by grade level. In S. Paynter, E. Bodrova, & J. Doty (Eds.), *For the love of words: Vocabulary instruction that works* (pp. 127–202). San Francisco, CA: Jossey Bass.

McDougal Littell. (2001). *Language network: Grammar, writing, communication 8.* Evanston, IL: Author.

McDougal Littell. (2006). *Creating America: A history of the United States (Beginnings through World War I)* (California ed.). Evanston, IL: Author.

McDougal Littell. (2007). *Science: Focus on physical science.* Evanston, IL: Author.

McKenna, M.C., & Stahl, S.A. (2009). *Assessment for reading instruction.* New York, NY: Guilford Press.

Nagy, W., Anderson, R.C., Schommer, M., Scott, J.A., & Stallman, A.C. (1989). Morphological families in the internal lexicon. *Reading Research Quarterly, 24*(3), 262–282.

Nation, I.S.P. (n.d.-a). *Range program with BNC/COCA lists 25,000.* Retrieved from http://www.victoria.ac.nz/lals/about/staff/paul-nation

Nation, I.S.P. (n.d.-b). *Vocabulary size test version A.* Retrieved from http://www.victoria.ac.nz/lals/about/staff/publications/paul-nation/VST-version-A.pdf

Nation, I.S.P. (1989). Improving speaking fluency. *System, 17*(3), 377–384.

Nation, I.S.P. (1990). *Teaching and learning vocabulary.* Boston, MA: Heinle and Heinle.

Nation, I.S.P. (1993). Measuring readiness for simplified material: A test of the first 1,000 words of English. In M.L. Tickoo (Ed.), *Simplification: Theory and application,* RELC Anthology Series 31 (pp. 193–203). Singapore: SEAMEO Regional Language Centre.

Nation, I.S.P. (2006). How large a vocabulary is needed for reading and listening? *The Canadian Modern Language Review, 63*(1), 59–82.

Nation, I.S.P. (2008). *Teaching vocabulary: Strategies and techniques.* Boston, MA: Heinle, CENGAGE Learning.

Nation, I.S.P. (2013). *Learning vocabulary in another language* (2nd ed.). Cambridge, United Kingdom: Cambridge University Press.

Nation, I.S.P., & Webb, S. (2011). *Researching and analyzing vocabulary.* Boston, MA: Heinle, CENGAGE Learning.

Nation, P. (2000). Learning vocabulary in lexical sets: Dangers and guidelines. *TESOL Journal, 9*(2), 6–10.

Nation, P. (2007). The four strands. *Innovation in language and teaching, 1*(1), 1–12.

Nation, P., & Beglar, D. (2007). A vocabulary size test. *The Language Teacher, 31*(7), 9–13.

Nation, P., & Coxhead, A. (2014). Vocabulary size research at Victoria University of Wellington, New Zealand. *Language Teaching, 47*(3), 398–403.

Nation, P., & Hwang, K. (1995). Where would general service vocabulary stop and special purposes vocabulary begin? *System, 23,* 35–41.

National Governors Association Center for Best Practices & Council of Chief State School Officers. (2010). *Common core state standards for English language arts &*

literacy in history/social studies, science, and technical subjects. Washington, DC: Author.

National Institute of Child Health and Human Development. (2000). *Report of the National Reading Panel. Teaching children to read: An evidence-based assessment of the scientific research literature on reading and its implications for reading instruction* (Comprehension Subgroup). Retrieved from http://www.nichd.nih.gov/publications/pubs/nrp/pages/report.aspx

Nguyen, L., & Nation, P. (2011). A bilingual vocabulary size test of English for Vietnamese learners. *RELC Journal, 42*(1), 86–99.

Nurweni, A., & Read, J. (1999). The English vocabulary knowledge of Indonesian university students. *English for Specific Purposes, 18*(2), 161–175.

Padilla, M., Miaoulis, I., & Cyr, M. (2005). *Science explorer: Physical science.* Upper Saddle River, NJ: Prentice Hall.

Pittelman, S.D. (1986). *Semantic mapping: Classroom applications.* Newark, DE: International Reading Association.

Rasinski, T. (2006). Developing vocabulary through word building. In C.C. Block & J.N. Mangieri (Eds.), *The vocabulary-enriched classroom: Practices for improving the reading performance of all students in grades 3 and up* (pp. 36–53). New York: Scholastic.

Schmitt, N. (2000). *Vocabulary in language teaching.* New York, NY: Cambridge University Press.

Schmitt, N. (2010). *Researching vocabulary: A vocabulary research manual.* New York, NY: Palgrave Macmillan.

Schmitt, N., & Schmitt, D. (2012). A reassessment of frequency and vocabulary size in L2 vocabulary teaching. *Language Teaching.* doi:10.1017/S0261444812000018.

Schmitt, N., Schmitt, D., & Clapham, C. (2001). Developing and exploring the behaviour of two new versions of the Vocabulary Levels Test. *Language Testing, 18*(1), 55–88.

Scott, J., Skobel, B.J., & Wells, J. (2008). *The word-conscious classroom: Building the vocabulary readers and writers need.* New York, NY: Scholastic.

Sinclair, J. (1999). *Corpus, concordance, collocation.* Oxford, United Kingdom: Oxford University Press.

Sinclair, J.M. (Ed.). (2003). *Collins cobuild advanced learner's English dictionary* (4th ed.). Glasgow, United Kingdom: Harper Collins.

Slavin, R.E. (1996). Research on cooperative learning and achievement: What we know, what we need to know. *Contemporary Educational Psychology, 21*(1), 43–69.

Snow, C., Lawrence, J., & White, C. (2009). Generating knowledge of academic language among urban middle school students. *Journal of Research on Educational Effectiveness, 2*(4), 325–344.

Stubbs, M. (1993). British traditions in text analysis: From Firth to Sinclair. In M. Baker, G. Francis, & E. Tognini-Bonelli (Eds.), *Text and technology: In honour of John Sinclair* (pp. 13–33). Amsterdam, Netherlands: John Benjamins.

Tompkins, G. (2014). *Literacy for the 21st century: A balanced approach.* Boston, MA: Pearson.

Wardhaugh, R. (2002). *An introduction to sociolinguistics* (4th ed.). Malden, MA: Blackwell.

West, M. (1953). *A general service list of English words.* London, United Kingdom: Longman.

Williams, K.T. (2006). *Expressive Vocabulary Test–Second Edition (EVT-2).* Bloomington, MN: American Guidance Service/Pearson.

Zwiers, J., O'Hara, S., & Pritchard, R. (2014). *Common core standards in diverse classrooms: Essential practices for developing academic language and disciplinary literacy.* Portland, ME: Stenhouse.

Appendix

The Middle School Vocabulary Lists

This Appendix presents the Middle School Vocabulary Lists. As discussed in prior chapters and in Appendix B, these are five lists, divided into the subject areas of English Grammar and Writing, Health, Mathematics, Science, and Social Studies and History. Each list shows the 300–400 word families that most frequently appear in middle school textbooks in those areas (see Appendix B; inclusion is based on a cutoff of overall frequency of use rather than a set total number).

The words are arranged in order of frequency of the word family. The most frequent family member is italicized. Usually, this is the headword (listed first/at left), but at times it is an alternate form of a word. Words that also appear on the AWL (Coxhead, 2000) are boldfaced.

MIDDLE SCHOOL ENGLISH
GRAMMAR AND WRITING VOCABULARY LIST

(sorted by family frequency)

Most-frequent family members are *italicized*. AWL words are **bolded.**

pronoun
  pronouns
phrase
  phrases
adjective

adjectives
paragraph
paragraphs
topic
topics

adverb
  adverbs
clause
  clauses
identify
  identified
  identifying
  identity
chapter
  chapters
compound
  compounds
preposition
  prepositional
  prepositions
modify
  modified
  modifier
  modifiers
  modifies
  modifying
predicate
  predicates
revise
  revised
  revising
  revision
  revisions
comma
  commas
create
  created
  creates
  creating
  creation
  creative
draft
  drafting
  drafts
essay

tense
  tenses
  tension
singular
underline
  underlined
conjunction
  conjunctions
error
  errors
quote
  quotation
  quotations
  quoted
  quotes
edit
  edited
  editing
  edition
  editor
  editorial
  editors
process
capitalize
  capitalization
  capitalized
section
  sections
define
  defined
  defines
  definition
  definitions
research
  researchers
  researching
participle
  participial
specific
  specifically

final
  finally
punctuate
  punctuation
conclude
  concluding
  conclusion
  conclusions
possessive
source
  sources
usage
author
  authors
movie
  movies
link
  linked
  linking
  links
instruct
  instruction
  instructional
  instructions
  instructor
team
  teams
compute
  computer
  computers
focus
  focused
  focuses
  focusing
item
  items
method
  methods
strategy
  strategies

online
rewrite
  rewriting
chart
  charts
tradition
  traditional
  traditions
period
  periodical
  periodicals
  periods
concept
  concepts
label
  labeled
  labels
publish
  published
  publisher
  publishing
parenthesis
  parentheses
assign
  assigned
  assignment
  assignments
definite
  definitely
  indefinite
evaluate
  evaluated
  evaluating
  evaluation
  evaluations
job
  jobs
fragment
  fragments
narrate

narrative
internet
transit
  transition
  transitional
  transitions
prewrite
  prewriting
area
  areas
classmate
  classmates
dialogue
media
site
  sites
style
  styles
communicate
  communicable
  communicating
  communication
  communications
image
  imagery
  images
similar
  similarities
  similarly
reference
apostrophe
  apostrophes
respond
  responded
  responding
  response
  responses
feature
  featured
  features

analyze
analysis
analyzing
locate
located
location
locations
workshop
negate
  negative
  negatives
select
  selected
  selection
  selects
structure
  structures
logic
  logical
  logically
journal
  journals
subordinate
interject
  interjection
  interjections
complement
  complements
principal
complex
element
  elements
goal
  goals
appositive
code
  codes
appropriate
contrast
  contrasting

contrasts
indicate
  indicated
  indicates
illustrate
  illustrated
  illustrates
  illustration
  illustrations
series
proofread
  proofreading
available
summary
  summarize
  summarizes
  summarizing
portfolio
infinitive
video
brief
  briefly
partner
interrogative
guideline
  guidelines
superlative
visual
  visualize
  visually
require
  required
  requires
affect
  affected
  affects
technical
coordinate
  coordinating
antecedent

project
  projects
vary
  varied
  varying
blank
checklist
text
precise
issue
  issues
demonstrate
  demonstrates
  demonstrative
museum
conflict
occur
  occurred
  occurs
design
  designed
  designs
function
  functional
  functions
technique
  techniques
kid
  kids
involve
  involved
  involving
  involves
vivid
standardize
  standardized
gerund
emphasis
  emphasize
  emphasizes

emphatic
consist
  consistent
  consistently
  consists
  inconsistent
nominative
physical
  physically
tone
column
major
electronic
expert
  experts
encyclopedia
positive
interpret
  interpretation
  interpreting
invert
  inverted
huge
catalog
feedback
community
  communities
grade
  graded
  grades
evident
  evidence
exclaim
  exclamation
peer
abbreviate
  abbreviation
  abbreviations
sensory
category

categories
plot
oral
novel
sequence
  sequential
contraction
  contractions
index
  indexes
verbal
culture
  cultural
  cultures
informative
interview
workbook
display
  displayed
  displays
eliminate
  eliminating
convince
  convincing
symbol
  symbols
passive
precede
  preceded
  preceding
challenge
  challenged
  challenges
  challenging
drama
  dramatic
technology
theme
  themes
highlight

highlighted
highlighting
highlights
react
  reaction
  reactions
instance
document
  documentation
  documents
aid
  aids
adult
  adults
region
  regional
  regions
thesis
comment
  comments
professional
role
  roles
version
  versions
overall
survive
  survival
  survived
assess
  assessment
equip
  equipment
accurate
  accurately
resource
  resources
energy
  energetic
injure

injured
injuries
individual
individuals
objective
access
  accessed
  accessible
intense
  intensive
insert
  inserting
benefit
  benefits
aspect
  aspects
environment
  environmental
percent
  percentage
format
option
  options
civil
interact
  interactive
tape
unique
target
file
  files
normal
  normally
schedule
mental
  mentally
construct
  constructed
  construction
context

resolve
  resolved
  resolution
academy
  academic
parallel
stress
remove
  removed
expand
  expanded
  expanding
rely
  reliable
attach
  attached
device
  devices
voluntary
  volunteer
  volunteers
infer
  inferences
cite
  cited
  citing
  citation
  citations
coherent
  coherence
clarify
  clarity
predict
  predictions
previous
achieve
criteria
medical
appreciate
  appreciation

approach
  approached
perspective
reveal
  reveals
abstract
mode
  modes
sum
  sums
contact
intelligence
  intelligent
route
vehicle
  vehicles
plus
statistic
  statistics
eventual
  eventually
publication
contemporary
contribute
  contributes
establish
  established
analogy
  analogies
range
conduct
  conducting
layer
  layers
obvious
  obviously
constant
  constantly
transport
  transportation

volume
immigrate
  immigrants
gender
relax
  relaxed
aware
enormous
data
classic
  classical
exhibit
impact
legal
  illegal
revolution
  revolutionary
manual
  manuals
shift
  shifts
task
founded
concentrate
purchase
  purchased
consequent
  consequence
  consequences
  consequently
imply
  implied
consume
  consumer
incidence
  incident
somewhat
debate
credit
confer

conference
convene
  convention
  conventions
attitude
automate
  automatic
  automatically
medium
occupy
  occupation
  occupations
accompany
  accompanied
abandon
  abandoned
release
  released
generate
  generating
  generation
  generations
substitute
adapt
  adapted
submit
chemical
  chemicals
lecture
principle
institute
  institutions
insight
ensure
military
outcome
primary
adequate
  adequately
encounter

participate
assume
correspond
  corresponding
visible
couple
margin
uniform
approximate
  approximately
reside
  resident
  residents
significant
vision
consult
detect
  detective
factor
  factors
constitute
  constitution
despite
portion
enhance
labor
maintain
potential
mature
panel
survey
assemble
  assembly
devote
foundation
minor

nevertheless
seek
theory
unify
  unified
channel
confirm
decade
federal
flexible
grant
likewise
relevant
globe
bias
internal
annual
authority
fee
proceed
promote
specify
  specified
adjust
core
ignorant
  ignorance
  ignore
  ignored
  ignores
neutral
odd
assist
  assistant
furthermore
monitor

MIDDLE SCHOOL HEALTH VOCABULARY LIST

(sorted by family frequency)

Most-frequent family members are *italicized*. AWL words are **bolded**.

drug
  drugs
physical
  physically
alcohol
  alcoholism
stress
  stressed
  stressful
  stressor
  stressors
goal
  goals
teen
  teens
affect
  affected
  affecting
  affects
  affection
emotion
  emotions
  emotional
healthful
injure
  injured
  injuries
  injury
adult
  adulthood
  adults
chapter
  chapters
conflict
  conflicts
infect

infected
infection
infections
infectious
noninfectious
muscle
  muscles
  muscular
cell
  cells
concept
  conception
  concepts
identify
  identified
  identifies
  identifying
  identity
communicate
  communicable
  communicating
  communication
cancer
  cancers
vocabulary
environment
  environmental
  environments
sex
  sexual
  sexually
abuse
  abused
positive
  positively
source

sources
pollute
  pollutants
  polluted
  pollution
diet
  dietary
  diets
peer
  peers
guideline
  guidelines
nutrient
  nutrients
disorder
  disorders
energy
  energetic
mental
  mentally
evaluate
  evaluating
area
  areas
aid
  aids
role
  roles
community
  communities
symptom
  symptoms
respond
  responding
  responds
  response
  responses
image
  images
legal

illegal
illegally
legally
esteem
victim
  victims
negate
  negative
  negatively
bacterium
  bacteria
  bacterial
emergency
  emergencies
nerve
  nervous
  nerves
medical
consume
  consumed
  consumer
  consumers
  consumes
  consumption
addict
  addicted
  addiction
  addictive
chemical
  chemicals
maintain
  maintained
  maintaining
  maintains
  maintenance
guardian
  guardians
factor
  factors
percent

percentage
analyze
  analysis
  analyzing
function
  functioning
  functions
virus
  viruses
  viral
physician
  physicians
occur
  occurs
require
  required
  requirements
  requires
label
  labeled
  labels
involve
  involved
  involvement
  involves
  involving
summary
  summarize
pregnant
  pregnancy
team
  teams
process
  processed
  processes
normal
  abnormal
  abnormally
  normally
tissue

tissues
hormone
  hormones
calorie
  calories
pathogen
  pathogens
abstain
  abstinence
depress
  depression
  depressed
react
  reaction
  reactions
  reacts
contact
resource
  resources
cigarette
  cigarettes
resolve
  resolution
  resolved
  resolving
benefit
  beneficial
  benefits
vitamin
  vitamins
cope
  coping
prescribe
  prescription
oxygen
research
  researchers
  researching
adolescent
  adolescence

adolescents
consequent
  consequence
  consequences
immune
remove
  removed
  removes
  removing
gland
  glands
digest
  digestion
  digestive
promote
  promotes
  promoting
reproductive
internet
allergy
  allergic
  allergies
media
quit
  quitting
ad
  ads
nicotine
focus
  focused
  focuses
  focusing
nutrition
vegetable
  vegetables
unhealthy
period
  periods
classmate
  classmates

respire
  respiratory
journal
item
  items
voluntary
  volunteer
  volunteering
  volunteers
participate
  participant
  participants
  participating
rely
  reliability
  reliable
  relies
diabetes
contract
  contracting
  contracts
healthcare
asthma
topic
  topics
graph
  graphic
career
  careers
professional
  professionals
marijuana
recover
  recovering
  recovery
counsel
  counseling
  counselor
  counselors
design

designed
designer
designing
chronic
release
  released
  releases
endure
  endurance
carbon
inhale
  inhalants
  inhaled
pyramid
achieve
  achieved
  achievement
  achieving
dependence
magazine
  magazines
antibiotic
  antibiotics
protein
  proteins
distress
equip
  equipment
influenza
  flu
relax
  relaxation
  relaxed
  relaxes
  relaxing
puberty
major
gang
  gangs
available

code
similar
  similarities
urine
  urinary
transmit
  transmission
  transmitted
specific
abdomen
  abdominal
fetus
sperm
tolerate
  tolerant
  tolerance
assess
  assessing
  assessment
lifestyle
wellness
option
  options
expose
  exposed
  exposure
medication
  medications
carbohydrate
  carbohydrates
demonstrate
  demonstrates
  demonstrating
individual
  individuals
site
  sites
fluid
  fluids
circulate

circulatory
cycle
  cycling
infer
  inference
  inferences
flexible
  flexibility
liver
stimulate
  stimulant
  stimulants
chart
  charts
create
  created
  creating
  creative
spine
  spinal
skeleton
  skeletal
mediate
  mediation
  mediator
range
define
challenge
  challenges
  challenging
culture
  cultural
  cultures
contribute
  contributes
conserve
  conservation
job
  jobs
cord

uterus
partner
  partners
strategy
  strategies
appropriate
  inappropriate
select
  selected
  selecting
  selection
layer
  layers
concentrate
  concentrating
  concentration
withdraw
  withdrawal
endocrine
compute
  computer
  computers
mood
valid
dental
locate
  located
  location
  locations
task
  tasks
heredity
project
  projects
trait
  traits
contrast
target
germ
  germs

vision
seek
  seeking
aware
  awareness
psychology
  psychological
  psychologically
cardiovascular
online
television
vehicle
  vehicles
conclude
  conclusion
  conclusions
ingredient
  ingredients
column
mature
  immature
  matures
  maturity
trigger
  triggered
  triggers
acne
myth
calcium
issue
  issues
purchase
  purchased
  purchases
  purchasing
commit
  commitment
  commitments
  committed
regulate

regulates
regulations
surgery
soccer
suicide
syndrome
dioxide
convince
  convincing
bloodstream
access
grade
  grades
coach
organizer
structure
  structures
cholesterol
cocaine
household
monoxide
method
  methods
final
  finally
mechanism
  mechanisms
detect
  detected
  detector
  detectors
intestine
dispose
  disposable
  disposal
  disposed
  disposing
enable
  enables
facilitate

facility
facilities
instruct
instruction
instructions
attitude
attitudes
attach
attached
attaches
minor
minors
overall
coordinate
coordination
visual
intense
intensity
technology
federal
advocate
proceed
procedure
procedures
internal
device
devices
predict
predictions
unpredictable
eventual
eventually
index
transport
transportation
transports
link
linked
paragraph
schedule

interpret
interpreting
survive
survival
technique
techniques
vary
varies
ensure
portion
portions
indicate
indicates
illustrate
tense
tension
sequence
adjust
adjusted
text
interact
interactions
complex
accurate
accuracy
authority
authorities
assist
assistance
external
eliminate
eliminates
alter
alternative
alternatives
consist
consists
constant
constantly
deny

denial
ignorance
  ignorant
  ignore
  ignoring
policy
  policies
style
  styles
approach
  approaches
  approaching
data
gender
cooperate
  cooperation
intervene
  intervention
potential
  potentially
feature
  features
survey
supplement
  supplements
administrate
  administration
category
  categories
primary
conduct
  conducts
estimate
  estimated
secure
  security
  insecurity
display
brief
  briefly

outcome
  outcomes
comment
  comments
visible
  invisible
expert
  experts
tradition
  traditions
  traditional
monitor
  monitoring
license
  licensed
labor
impact
obtain
route
  routes
globe
  global
finance
  financial
statistic
  statistics
section
tape
academy
  academic
maximize
  maximum
income
series
unique
institute
  institutes
aspect
  aspects
consent

status
significant
  significantly
volume
component
  components
consult
temporary
adequate
network
passive
priority
  priorities
couple
credit
element
  elements
circumstance
  circumstances
principle
  principles
annual
establish
obvious
medium
restore
trace
minimum
  minimize
instance
acquire
  acquired
encounter
ethnic
fee
nuclear
convert
  converts
domestic
assign

assignments
adapt
commission
enforce
integrity
previous
diverse
  diversity
assume
framework
occupy
  occupational
persist
  persistent
register
  registered
despite
mutual
ongoing
pose
practitioner
random
ratio
scenario
distort
  distorted
construct
  construction
evident
  evidence
motive
  motivate
accompany
appreciate
foundation
substitute
perceive
  perception
compound
  compounds

panel   *drama*
revise   *expand*
trend   *investigate*
bias   *neutral*
capable   *objective*

MIDDLE SCHOOL MATHEMATICS VOCABULARY LIST

(sorted by family frequency)

Most-frequent family members are *italicized*. AWL words are **bolded**.

equate
  equation
  equations
graph
  graphic
  graphing
  graphs
area
  areas
fraction
  fractional
  fractions
chapter
  chapters
data
triangle
  triangles
  triangular
percent
  percentage
  percents
decimal
  decimals
factor
  factored
  factoring
  factorization
  factors
mathematics
  math

mathematical
mathematician
mathematicians
meter
  centimeter
  centimeters
  kilometer
  kilometers
  meters
  metric
  millimeter
  millimeters
estimate
  estimated
  estimates
  estimating
  estimation
rectangle
  rectangles
  rectangular
subtract
  subtracted
  subtracting
  subtraction
integer
  integers
vary
  variable
  variables
  variation

varies

sum

  sums

algebra

  algebraic

function

  functions

volume

  volumes

height

cube

  cubes

  cubic

proportion

  proportional

  proportions

ratio

  ratios

coordinate

  coordinates

evaluate

  evaluating

formula

  formulas

  formulate

negate

  negative

perimeter

denominator

  denominators

exponent

  exponential

  exponents

rational

  irrational

positive

plot

  plots

prism

  prisms

linear

  nonlinear

similar

  similarity

  similarly

equivalent

  equivalents

score

  scored

  scores

dimension

  dimensional

  dimensions

vocabulary

geometry

  geometric

method

  methods

tile

  tiles

digit

  digits

identify

  identified

  identifies

  identifying

  identity

congruous

  congruence

  congruent

analyze

  analysis

  analyzing

polygon

  polygons

vertex

  vertices

sequence

  sequences

display

displayed
displaying
displays
diagram
prime
select
selected
selecting
selection
selections
selects
quotient
quotients
median
survey
surveyed
surveys
strategy
strategies
intercept
intercepts
team
teams
mental
mentally
axis
diameter
range
ranges
segment
segments
outcome
outcomes
cylinder
cylinders
polynomial
polynomials
substitute
substituted
substituting

substitution
label
labeled
labels
concept
concepts
symbol
symbolic
symbols
parallelogram
parallelograms
notate
notation
predict
predicted
prediction
predictions
inequalities
pyramid
pyramids
correspond
corresponds
corresponding
numerator
numerators
involve
involved
involves
involving
approximate
approximately
approximation
random
randomly
radius
convert
conversion
conversions
converting
item

items
circumference
compute
  computation
  computer
  computers
  computing
mode
homework
section
  sections
marble
  marbles
divisor
  divisible
  divisibility
justify
  justification
challenge
distribute
  distributed
  distribution
  distributive
parallel
vertical
error
  errors
appropriate
source
locate
  located
  location
  locations
create
  created
  creating
ounce
  ounces
project
grade

graders
symmetry
quadratic
rotate
  rotation
  rotational
  rotations
image
  images
link
cone
  cones
quiz
column
  columns
inverse
design
  designed
  designing
  designs
laboratory
  lab
construct
  constructed
  constructing
  construction
statistic
  statistical
  statistics
conclude
  conclusion
  conclusions
odd
  odds
trapezoid
  trapezoids
reciprocal
  reciprocals
input
  inputs

movie
  movies
quadrilateral
define
  defined
  definition
  definitions
  undefined
indicate
  indicated
  indicates
perpendicular
constant
plus
sketch
discount
transform
  transformation
  transformations
output
  outputs
spinner
region
  regions
grid
investigate
  investigating
  investigation
pizza
occur
  occurred
  occurring
  occurs
horizontal
rewrite
compass
cell
  cells
theorem
acute

goal
  goals
interval
  intervals
baseball
basketball
obtuse
purchase
  purchased
  purchases
counter
  counters
adult
  adults
process
  processes
compound
  compounded
respond
  response
  responses
online
complement
  complementary
chart
  charts
domain
previous
  previously
target
  targeted
remove
  removed
  removing
parenthesis
  parentheses
hypotenuse
calorie
  calories
period

periods
commutative
illustrate
  illustrated
  illustrates
  illustration
supplement
  supplementary
annual
  annually
objective
spreadsheet
theory
  theoretical
arithmetic
cumulative
maximize
  maximum
summary
  summarize
final
  finally
lateral
hint
tank
job
  jobs
keyword
requisite
  prerequisite
workbook
associative
require
  required
  requires
affect
  affected
  affects
assess
  assessment

bias
  biased
  unbiased
tape
  tapes
radical
  radicals
technology
capacity
available
eliminate
  eliminated
  elimination
assume
  assuming
principal
logic
  logical
trace
  tracing
sphere
  spheres
interpret
  interpreting
topic
  topics
simulate
  simulation
invest
  invested
  investment
option
  options
expand
  expanded
fee
sector
  sectors
income
principle

trend
  trends
accurate
  accuracy
  accurately
route
  routes
adjacent
compatible
generate
  generated
precise
  precision
terminate
  terminating
minimum
focus
reverse
  reversing
proceed
  procedure
  procedures
commission
research
element
  elements
layer
  layers
consume
  consumed
  consumer
category
  categories
portion
code
  codes
technique
  techniques
index
significant

vehicle
  vehicles
consist
  consists
site
resource
  resources
physical
partner
energy
initial
isolate
specific
journal
visual
  visualize
overlap
  overlapping
normal
complex
task
  tasks
demonstrate
medium
equip
  equipment
identical
alter
  alternate
voluntary
  volunteer
  volunteers
transport
  transportation
conduct
  conducted
assign
  assigned
obtain
  obtained

individual
file
fund
fundamental
maintain
  maintaining
document
major
converse
convince
  convincing
exclude
  exclusive
finite
  infinite
  infinitely
mutual
  mutually
community
register
  registered
valid
revolution
  revolutions
credit
revise
attach
  attached
context
reside
  resident
  residents
drama
release
  released
series
hypothesis
occupy

occupied
instruct
  instruction
  instructions
exhibit
paragraph
communicate
network
perspective
insert
participate
feature
underlie
  underlying
schedule
approach
professional
instance
overall
format
successor
  successive
shift
guideline
  guidelines
structure
interact
  interactive
confirm
license
unique
text
theme
concentrate
labor
environment
contrast
adjust

MIDDLE SCHOOL SCIENCE VOCABULARY LIST

(sorted by family frequency)

Most-frequent family members are *italicized*. AWL words are **bolded.**

energy

cell

  cells

chapter

  chapters

organism

  organisms

atom

  atomic

  atoms

chemical

  chemically

  chemicals

area

  areas

data

section

  sections

element

  elements

concept

  concepts

  conceptual

process

  processes

  processing

react

  reaction

  reactions

  reactive

  reacts

volcano

  volcanic

  volcanoes

occur

  occurred

occurrence

occurring

occurs

layer

layered

layers

structure

structural

structures

carbon

affect

affected

affecting

affects

meter

  centimeters

  kilometers

  meters

  metric

molecule

  molecules

oxygen

resource

  resources

graph

  graphs

atmosphere

vocabulary

identify

  identification

  identified

  identifies

  identifying

  identity

planet

  planets

environment
  environmental
  environments
fossil
  fossils
dense
  density
hypothesis
  hypotheses
  hypothesize
  hypothesized
compound
  compounds
solar
locate
  located
  location
  locations
create
  created
  creates
  creating
  creative
current
  currents
period
  periodic
  periods
sediment
  sedimentary
  sediments
diagram
  diagrams
species
vary
  variable
  variables
  variation
  variations
  varies

varying
electron
  electrons
acid
  acids
volume
  volumes
predict
  predictable
  predicted
  predicting
  prediction
  predictions
function
  functioning
  functions
cycle
  cycles
similar
  similarities
  similarly
  simulate
gene
  genes
  genetic
gravity
  gravitational
analyze
  analysis
  analyzing
source
  sources
continent
  continents
  continental
muscle
  muscles
erode
  eroded
  erodes

eroding
erosion
physical
climate
climates
release
released
releases
releasing
investigate
investigating
investigation
investigations
tissue
tissues
ecosystem
ecosystems
factor
factors
bacterium
bacteria
image
images
conclude
concluded
conclusion
conclusions
trait
traits
hydrogen
bond
bonded
bonding
bonds
research
researchers
researching
ion
ionic
ions

infer
inference
inferences
inferring
chromosome
chromosomes
dioxide
percent
percentage
percentages
evident
evidence
region
regions
proceed
procedure
procedures
nucleus
fuel
fuels
theory
theories
laboratory
lab
assess
assessment
fluid
fluids
radiate
radiation
design
designed
designing
designs
galaxy
galaxies
crust
major
majority
protein

proteins
transfer
   transferred
   transfers
method
   methods
tectonic
   tectonics
select
   selected
   selection
   selective
allele
   alleles
magnet
   magnetic
   electromagnetic
magma
feature
   features
plastic
zone
interpret
   interpreting
   interprets
erupt
   eruption
   eruptions
range
   ranges
   ranging
remove
   removal
   removed
   removing
   removes
friction
contrast
   contrasting
label

labeled
labels
focus
   focused
   focuses
nerve
   nervous
journal
lens
nitrogen
telescope
   telescopes
pollute
   pollution
web
deposit
   deposits
   deposition
respond
   responding
   responds
   response
   responses
survive
   survival
   survived
geology
   geologic
accelerate
   acceleration
topic
   topics
offspring
sex
   sexual
   sexually
precipitate
   precipitation
adapt
   adaptation

adaptations
adapted
height
mathematics
  math
nutrient
  nutrients
define
  defined
  defining
  definition
  definitions
  definite
axis
glacier
  glaciers
orbit
mammal
  mammals
equate
  equation
  equations
velocity
proton
  protons
constant
  constantly
dissolve
  dissolved
mantle
interact
  interaction
  interactions
  interactive
  interacts
visible
  invisible
absorb
  absorbed
convert

conversion
conversions
converted
converting
converts
indicate
indicated
indicates
indicator
indicators
evolve
  evolved
  evolution
  evolutionary
normal
  normally
tiny
convection
globe
  global
core
  cores
photosynthesis
code
  codes
crystal
  crystals
illustrate
  illustrated
  illustrates
  illustration
  illustrations
fungus
  fungi
lava
astronomy
  astronomer
  astronomers
summary
  summarize

summarizes
summarizing
involve
  involved
  involves
  involving
microscope
communicate
  communicating
  communication
specific
vapor
neutron
  neutrons
individual
  individuals
chart
  charts
construct
  constructed
  constructing
  construction
formula
  formulas
  formulate
membrane
transport
  transportation
  transported
  transporting
  transports
site
  sites
consume
  consumed
  consumer
  consumers
thermal
technology
compute

computer
computers
humid
  humidity
role
  roles
igneous
sequence
  sequences
  sequencing
conduct
  conducted
  conducting
  conducts
tropic
  tropical
nuclear
kinetic
require
  required
  requires
challenge
latitude
balloon
sperm
concentrate
  concentrated
  concentration
beaker
equator
sodium
eventual
  eventually
tape
link
  linked
  links
community
  communities
internet

obtain
  obtained
  obtaining
conserve
  conservation
mercury
expand
  expanding
  expands
  expansion
symbol
  symbols
consist
  consistent
  consisting
  consists
seismic
handbook
rotate
  rotation
attach
  attached
  attaches
beach
negate
  negative
  negatively
magnitude
algae
aluminum
ratio
  ratios
project
  projection
  projections
  projects
respire
  respiration
positive
  positively

giant
complex
huge
organic
accurate
  accuracy
  accurately
column
diameter
polar
potential
paragraph
  paragraphs
adult
  adulthood
  adults
hemisphere
reptile
  reptiles
strategy
  strategies
radioactive
dominate
  dominant
channel
  channels
evaluate
  evaluating
checkpoint
groundwater
impact
  impacts
phase
  phases
helium
principle
  principles
cylinder
expose
  exposed

exposure
wavelength
stable
  unstable
final
  finally
thermometer
maintain
  maintaining
  maintains
lithosphere
generation
  generations
drift
spectrum
marine
available
primary
  primarily
internal
contour
metamorphic
vascular
estimate
  estimated
lever
displace
  displaced
  displacement
  displaces
rocket
item
  items
era
ozone
buoy
  buoyant
hurricane
elevate
  elevation

embryo
detect
  detected
jar
partner
medium
mirror
trace
  traces
  tracing
identical
benefit
  beneficial
  benefits
generate
  generated
  generates
distribute
  distributed
  distribution
device
  devices
transform
  transformations
  transformed
unique
contact
approximate
  approximately
contribute
  contributed
  contributes
  contributions
series
equip
  equipment
appropriate
contract
  contracts
instruct

instruction
instructions
goal
goals
index
visual
visualization
visualizing
stress
team
teams
display
displays
category
categories
input
intense
intensity
job
jobs
sphere
spheres
spherical
transmit
transmission
transmitted
academy
academic
external
injure
injury
injured
injuries
component
components
successor
succession
diverse
diversity
revolution

undergo
undergoes
alter
alternate
alternating
alternative
output
parallel
reverse
reversals
vehicle
vehicles
vision
tense
tension
interval
intervals
phenomenon
phenomena
enable
enables
approach
approaches
approaching
aid
aids
neutral
append
appendix
differentiate
differentiation
consequent
consequence
consequences
previous
previously
proportion
proportional
proportions
apparent

portion
rely
  reliable
target
capacity
demonstrate
brief
  briefly
suspend
  suspended
  suspension
mature
objective
integrate
  integration
significant
modify
  modified
overall
mechanism
  mechanisms
technique
  techniques
enormous
domain
  domains
distinct
flexible
maximize
  maximum
regulate
  regulates
transit
  transition
medical
task
  tasks

derive
  derived
metamorphosis
adjust
  adjustment
rigid
text
trend
  trends
dispose
  disposal
depress
  depression
  depressions
collapse
shift
reveal
  revealed
trigger
  triggered
initial
plus
revise
parameter
  parameters
network
instance
annual
virtual
establish
  established
issue
  issues
incline
  inclined
grade
voluntary

volunteer
assume
framework
insert
prior
capable
monitor
culture
  cultures
publish
  published
precise
despite
prime
dimension
  dimensions
obvious
dynamic
highlight
  highlighted
minor
secure
passive
logic
  logical
error
isolate
  isolated
manipulate
  manipulated
somewhat
migrate
overlap
complement
  complementary
terminate
  terminal

option
  optional
ensure
substitute
decade
  decades
eliminate
guideline
  guidelines
exhibit
outcome
survey
acquire
  acquired
incidence
relax
valid
equivalent
drama
  dramatic
sum
accumulate
encounter
uniform
liberal
  liberate
random
adjacent
margin
debate
whereas
occupy
statistic
  statistics
version
likewise
recover

MIDDLE SCHOOL SOCIAL STUDIES AND HISTORY VOCABULARY LIST

(sorted by family frequency)

Most-frequent family members are *italicized*. AWL words are **bolded**.

chapter
  chapters
economy
  economic
  economically
  economics
  economies
section
  sections
region
  regional
  regions
culture
  cultural
  cultures
area
  areas
create
  created
  creates
  creating
  creation
  creative
  creator
constitute
  constitution
  constitutional
  constitutions
  unconstitutional
major
  majority
congress
  congressional
identify
  identified
  identifying

identity
source
  sources
locate
  located
  location
  locations
revolution
  revolutionaries
  revolutionary
  revolutions
analyze
  analysis
  analyzing
geography
  geographic
civil
goods
issue
  issued
  issues
affect
  affected
  affects
troop
  troops
summary
  summaries
  summarize
  summarizing
democracy
  democratic
immigrate
  immigrant
  immigrants
  immigration

resource
 resources
territory
 territories
chart
 charts
amend
 amendment
 amendments
establish
 established
 establishes
 establishing
 establishment
federal
 federation
military
civilization
 civilizations
research
 researching
climate
 climates
expand
 expanded
 expanding
 expands
 expansion
conclude
 concluded
 conclusion
 conclusions
conflict
 conflicts
job
 jobs
define
 defined
 defining
 definition

definitions
role
 roles
construct
 constructed
 construction
 reconstruction
primary
 primarily
technology
 technological
tradition
 traditional
 traditions
interpret
 interpretation
 interpretations
 interpreting
policy
 policies
legislate
 legislature
 legislation
 legislative
 legislators
continent
 continental
community
 communities
graph
 graphic
period
 periods
environment
 environmental
 environments
reform
 reforms
assess
 assessment

percent
  percentage
vocabulary
grant
  granted
  granting
  grants
feature
  featured
  features
contrast
  contrasting
  contrasts
treaty
challenge
  challenged
  challenges
final
  finally
route
  routes
convene
  convention
  conventions
export
  exported
  exports
site
  sites
physical
web
contribute
  contributed
  contribution
  contributions
mission
  missions
emperor
fort
internet

similar
  similarities
paragraph
  paragraphs
founded
  founders
  founding
labor
link
  linked
  linking
  links
infer
  inference
  inferences
senate
supreme
capture
  captured
code
  codes
project
  projects
  projection
  projections
topic
  topics
interact
  interaction
  interactive
transport
  transportation
  transported
process
  processes
  processing
significant
  significance
respond
  responded

response
responses
huge
achieve
  achieved
  achievement
  achievements
individual
  individuals
dynasty
delegate
  delegates
goal
  goals
require
  required
  requirements
  requires
rebel
  rebellion
survive
  survival
  survived
  survivors
benefit
  benefited
  benefits
theme
  thematic
  themes
compromise
document
  documents
enslave
  enslaved
authority
  authorities
eventual
  eventually
structure

structures
involve
  involved
  involvement
  involves
strategy
  strategies
design
  designed
  designs
port
  ports
focus
  focused
ethnic
frontier
factor
  factors
debate
  debated
  debates
globe
  global
  globalization
method
  methods
impact
migrate
  migrated
  migration
  migrations
quote
  quotation
  quoted
legal
  illegal
organizer
diagram
visual
  visualize

image
images
gulf
evaluate
evaluating
occur
occurred
occurs
buffalo
era
remove
removal
removed
journal
parliament
symbol
symbols
seek
seeking
sought
citizenship
peninsula
assemble
assembled
assemblies
assembly
despite
expedition
range
ranges
text
texts
item
items
ally
allies
recall
county
sequence
sequencing

historians
evident
evidence
illustrate
illustrated
illustrates
illustration
illustrations
communist
rural
aid
aided
aids
preview
depress
depression
principle
principles
urban
style
styles
trail
online
executive
fertile
label
labeled
labels
predict
predicted
predictions
select
selected
selection
publish
published
publishing
navy
philosophy
philosopher

philosophers
campaign
tense
  tension
  tensions
maintain
  maintained
  maintaining
diverse
  diversity
author
  authors
purchase
  purchased
decline
  declined
series
enforce
  enforced
  enforcement
minor
  minorities
  minority
brief
  briefly
adapt
  adapted
equip
  equipped
  equipment
secure
  security
drama
  dramatic
  dramatically
rely
  reliable
  relied
promote
  promoted

draft
  drafted
  drafting
voluntary
  volunteer
  volunteers
communicate
  communication
  communications
reside
  resident
  residents
option
  options
institute
  institution
  institutions
category
  categories
  categorizing
participate
  participated
  participation
available
occupy
  occupation
  occupied
energy
fund
  funds
  funding
convince
  convinced
cooperate
  cooperation
  cooperative
commission
  commissioner
  commissioners
appropriate

approximate
approximately
aspect
aspects
specific
guarantee
guaranteed
guarantees
compute
computer
computers
accurate
accuracy
accurately
invest
invested
investors
investment
resolve
resolved
resolution
emerge
emerged
emergence
finance
financial
regulate
regulation
regulations
classic
classical
edit
editor
edited
editorial
react
reacted
reaction
reactions
convert

converted
converts
collapse
collapsed
theory
theories
complex
discriminate
discrimination
income
partner
partners
data
decade
decades
isolate
isolated
isolation
isolationism
medical
neutral
neutrality
vary
varied
varies
radical
radicals
conduct
conducted
consequent
consequence
consequences
deny
denied
generation
generations
administrate
administration
reject
rejected

restore
  restored
element
  elements
prime
network
  networks
clarify
  clarifying
domestic
  domesticated
abandon
  abandoned
contract
  contracts
dominate
  dominant
  dominated
clause
monitor
  monitoring
technique
  techniques
distribute
  distributed
  distribution
team
  teams
concept
  concepts
previous
  previously
task
overseas
consist
  consisted
  consists
attitude
  attitudes
chemical

chemicals
corporate
  corporation
  corporations
ignorance
  ignorant
  ignore
  ignored
approach
  approached
restrict
  restricted
  restrictions
display
  displayed
stable
  stability
estate
  estates
status
consume
  consumer
  consumers
bias
nuclear
unique
distinct
  distinctive
devote
  devoted
  devotion
trace
prohibit
  prohibited
  prohibition
layer
  layers
expert
  experts
acquire

acquired

consent

release

   released

thesis

unify

   unified

contact

bond

   bonds

alternative

academy

   academic

access

enable

   enabled

constant

   constantly

adult

   adults

estimate

   estimated

currency

widespread

obtain

   obtained

shift

   shifted

reveal

   revealed

impose

   imposed

logic

   logical

outcome

assign

   assigned

   assignment

emphasis

   emphasized

integrate

   integrated

mental

   mentally

trend

   trends

error

   errors

welfare

assist

   assistance

violate

   violated

foundation

commit

   committed

internal

cycle

framework

intelligence

   intelligent

instruct

   instruction

   instructions

indicate

positive

negate

   negative

file

media

controversy

   controversial

facilitate

   facility

   facilities

enormous

ensure

credit

target

statistic

statistics
relevant
transform
  transformed
function
  functions
device
  devices
pursue
  pursuit
revenue
encounter
  encountered
instance
successor
  succession
motive
  motives
erode
  erosion
context
transit
  transition
innovate
  innovations
grade
justify
  justified
overall
professional
consult
  consultation
portion
revise
parallel
confer
  conference
temporary
channel
vehicle

vehicles
fundamental
accompany
  accompanied
vision
annual
version
highlight
  highlighted
stress
  stressed
perspective
attach
  attached
injure
  injured
nevertheless
potential
reinforce
  reinforcements
demonstrate
principal
circumstance
  circumstances
sole
expose
  exposed
incidence
  incident
aware
uniform
guideline
  guidelines
couple
detect
evolve
  evolved
prior
liberal
recover

pose   **correspond**
core   *correspondence*
tape   *capable*
margin   *transfer*
intense   *exhibit*
investigate   *fee*
virtual   *normal*
eliminate   *alter*
register

Appendix

Methodology for the Compilation of the Middle School Vocabulary Lists

In this appendix, we describe the creation of a corpus of textbooks used by middle school students, as well as how the Middle School Vocabulary Lists were derived from that corpus and the process used to evaluate the lists. On the surface, the process of vocabulary identification in corpus-based research seems quite simple: first, gather a collection of texts; next, scan them into text files; and finally, use word-counting software to determine the most frequently occurring words. Things are never as simple as they seem, however, so in the next section we provide a brief discussion of the principles and considerations that corpus researchers keep in mind to guide the process of corpus development.

PRINCIPLES AND CONSIDERATIONS FOR CORPUS DEVELOPMENT

The first step in corpus-based research is the planning and creation of a corpus. Over the years, researchers have developed conventions for the creation of a principled corpus. In a discussion of the traditions used in text analysis, Stubbs (1993) described principles for corpus development considered essential to linguistic study. Three of these principles are directly related to the corpus designer's decisions. First, Stubbs declared that researchers must study authentically occurring language as it is used in real life. Stubbs's second principle insisted that complete texts be used in the research, as opposed to selections of text. Finally, Stubbs noted that texts and text types should be studied comparatively across corpora. The point here is that there are differences in language use, and different texts will contain different kinds of vocabulary (see Nation & Webb, 2011, Chapter 8, for more on making word lists using corpora).

In addition to Stubbs's principles, Hunston (2002) described four specific areas for consideration when designing a corpus: size, content, balance and representativeness, and permanence. Size, the first area of consideration, is important, because bigger is not always better, but sometimes it is; a larger corpus can help assure a researcher of enough data to support a conclusion. At the same time, researchers need to be sure that their computer software can handle the amount of data being processed, and that the information provided will not be too overwhelming for a researcher.

The next consideration is one of content. What types of texts should a corpus designer select? Should they be spoken or written? From what genres? Marzano (2004) brought up a concern that a corpus designer would use an inappropriate corpus to create a word list (e.g., use a corpus of auto repair manuals to create a list of academic words for K–12 students). Hunston (2002) noted that decisions in this area are made with the research question in hand. For example, if a teacher wanted to know the most frequently used words in the novels that students would be reading in class, he or she would purposely select those novels for the class's corpus. To study the language used by teachers in a classroom, a researcher would record teachers talking to their classes, transcribe it word for word, and use those transcripts for the corpus. To find the most frequently occurring words contained in sixth-grade science textbooks, a researcher would collect sixth-grade science textbooks for the corpus. In other words, the purpose of the research shapes the decisions regarding the content of the corpus.

The next areas for consideration are balance and representativeness. If a corpus is designed to represent a specific kind of language (e.g., academic writing), then the corpus needs to equally represent the different areas of academic writing that occur. The final consideration is one of permanence. If a corpus is created and left as is, then at some point it will no longer reflect authentic language. As an example, a corpus of spoken English from Shakespeare's day would be very different from a corpus of spoken English from the 21st century. On the other hand, continuous additions to a corpus require significant time, energy, and financial resources. Therefore, considerations regarding permanence are decided by how a corpus is meant to be used. If a corpus designer wants to study changes in language use over time, then the corpus must be continually updated; if not, then the updating process is not important.

Clearly, there is a great deal to consider when designing a corpus for linguistic research, and researchers face tensions within and between these areas when making decisions about text selections for corpus study. Keeping these considerations in mind, we describe the development of the MS-CAT Corpus in the next section.

THE MIDDLE SCHOOL CONTENT-AREA TEXTBOOK CORPUS

The MS-CAT Corpus is composed of content-area textbooks used by middle school students in public schools in the United States. The selection of texts depended upon two criteria: 1) the subject matter of the textbook, and 2) the grade level suggested by the publisher for a particular textbook. First, a textbook was required to be representative of the subject matter of English grammar and writing, health, mathematics, science, or social studies and history. Reading and literature textbooks were purposely excluded: although reading and literature textbooks contain instructional text, they are predominantly filled with fictional text, which is a different genre from academic text and therefore not appropriate for a corpus of academic textbooks. Second, a textbook had to be written for students at the sixth-, seventh-, or eighth-grade levels. The MS-CAT Corpus is composed of 109 content-area textbooks from the content areas of English grammar and writing, health, mathematics, science, and social studies and history. The purposeful selection of content-area textbooks used by middle school students was done with Hunston's (2002) considerations for content, balance, and representativeness, as well as the research questions, in mind. Table B.1 describes the textbook composition of the MS-CAT Corpus by content area and grade level.

The written content of each source textbook (omitting tables of contents and other front matter, and appendices, glossaries, and other back matter) was scanned into a text file. Individual text files were then numbered and filed according to content area and grade level. This methodology meets Stubbs's (1993) principles of using authentically occurring language

Table B.1. Textbook composition of the Middle School Content-Area Textbook Corpus

	Content area					
	English grammar and writing	Health	Math	Science	Social studies and history	Total
6th Grade	6	3	12	9	9	39
7th Grade	7	2	9	7	8	33
8th Grade	5	2	14	7	9	37
Number of texts	18	7	35	23	26	109

(i.e., the language contained in the textbooks) as well as using entire texts for corpus study. The next step involved sorting the files into subcorpora by content area and grade level. This step provided the opportunity to study the language contained in the texts comparatively across corpora, which is the third of Stubbs's principles. The MS-CAT Corpus contains more than 18 million running words of text, which is a reasonably sized corpus.

Table B.2 describes the number of running words in the MS-CAT Corpus by content area and grade level. A quick glance at the bottom line shows that the numbers of words are not evenly balanced between the subcorpora. There are two reasons for this. First, there are more textbooks available for some content areas than others (e.g., there just are not as many health textbooks as there are science or history texts). Also, some textbooks contain more words than others. The social studies and history subcorpus is composed of 26 textbooks and the math subcorpus contains 35 textbooks, yet the math subcorpus contains more than a half million fewer running words than the social studies and history subcorpus. The variations in size of the subcorpora were accounted for in the word selection process, and we describe that process later in this appendix. The final consideration in the design of the MS-CAT Corpus was one of permanence (Hunston, 2002). A permanent corpus was appropriate for this study because the research questions did not include the investigation of changes in textbook language use over time.

In this section, we described the creation of the MS-CAT Corpus and its five content-area subcorpora, and situated its development within the principles and considerations surrounding corpus-based research as described by Stubbs (1993) and Hunston (2002). In the next section, we explain the identification of the words on the Middle School Vocabulary Lists, which were derived from this corpus.

Table B.2.   Running word composition of the Middle School Content-Area Textbook Corpus

	Number of running words by content area and grade level					
	English grammar and writing	Health	Math	Science	Social studies and history	Total
6th Grade	811,647	333,468	1,680,737	1,330,662	1,754,229	5,910,743
7th Grade	1,164,185	232,062	1,283,934	1,181,148	1,744,301	5,605,630
8th Grade	957,525	347,313	2,067,089	1,213,612	2,100,470	6,686,009
Running words	2,933,357	912,843	5,031,760	3,725,422	5,599,000	18,202,382

DEVELOPMENT OF THE MIDDLE SCHOOL VOCABULARY LISTS

The MS-CAT Corpus was created to identify the most frequently occurring academic vocabulary contained in the corpus. The word identification process included a purposeful selection of words on the AWL (Coxhead, 2000). Middle school students will need to know these words to begin preparing for the rigors of university-level coursework; therefore, it made good sense to find out which of those words occurred frequently in middle school content-area textbooks. In the next subsection, we briefly describe the development of the AWL, because the Middle School Vocabulary Lists were developed using much the same methodology.

Development of the Academic Word List

Coxhead (2000) wanted to identify the academic vocabulary that students working toward university-level study would frequently encounter. She began the process with the creation of the Academic Corpus, which is a written corpus of university-level academic texts. The Academic Corpus contains 3,513,330 running words, which are referred to as *tokens,* and is divided into four subcorpora representing the disciplines of arts, commerce, law, and science. Coxhead had three criteria for the primary identification of words on the AWL. First, identified words could not be high-frequency words, and for this reason she excluded words from the GSL (West, 1953). Second, the words had to have a range of occurrence; that is, they had to occur at least 10 times within each of the four discipline-area subcorpora. Third, words had to occur with a minimum frequency of 100 times in the Academic Corpus.

The next step was to organize the identified words into families. In each word family there is a headword, which is the base stem of a word that can stand as a free form. Coxhead used the words *special* and *specify* as examples. In this case, *spec* would not be the base stem of these words, because it cannot stand on its own as a word, so *special* and *specify* would instead be their own headwords. Family members include inflected forms as well as prefixes and suffixes as defined by Bauer and Nation (1993) Level 6. This procedure provided three benefits. First, there is evidence that word families are stored as units in the mental lexicon (Nagy, Anderson, Schommer, Scott, & Stallman, 1989). Second, this controlled selection allows for standardization throughout the AWL and provides learners the opportunities to see word-building patterns. Finally, learners who know a base word's meaning and understand the ways in which inflections and affixes add to its meaning will have an easier time discerning the meanings of related family members.

The resulting AWL contains 570 word families and covers 10% of the running words in the Academic Corpus (see Coxhead [2000] for a full discussion of the methodology used to create the AWL). Since its publication in 2000, the AWL is arguably the most well-known list of academic vocabulary available. It has consistently been shown to do exactly what it was meant to do, which is to provide good coverage across a range of university-level academic texts from multiple disciplines. It is interesting to note that this broad coverage is also the primary criticism directed toward it, in that it is too broad and does not provide consistent coverage of discipline-specific texts (Davies & Gardner, 2013; Hyland & Tse, 2007; Martinez, Beck, & Panza, 2009). This being said, Nation (2013) pointed out that there is value in knowing the common words used across a range of academic texts. AWL words are primarily supportive in nature, and their meanings are not easily understood; however, knowing their meanings helps to provide access to the genre of academic writing (see Nation, 2013, pp. 293–295 for a full discussion of these ideas).

In this subsection, we described the development of the AWL and discussed some of the criticisms associated with it. In the next section, we demonstrate the presence of AWL and GSL words in the MS-CAT Corpus.

Presence of General Service List and Academic Word List Words in the Middle School Content-Area Textbook Corpus

The first step in the analysis of the MS-CAT Corpus was to determine its vocabulary profile, which shows the presence of high-frequency words from the GSL (West, 1953) and the AWL (Coxhead, 2000), as well as the text coverage these words provide. Because the MS-CAT Corpus is a corpus of written texts for middle school students, it was reasonable to expect some differences between the vocabulary in this corpus and the vocabulary contained in Coxhead's Academic Corpus, a corpus of written texts for students working toward university-level study.

The software program Range 1.32 (Heatley, Nation, & Coxhead, 2002) was used for this study, because it is powerful enough to handle an 18-million-word corpus and also provides the capability to determine word frequency, both within a single text and across multiple texts. In addition, it can be set to identify or ignore specific words. As an example, Range can be set to look for AWL words as well as GSL words, and it will provide a report that lists each of the words and their frequency of use within the texts.

Range analysis showed that GSL words represented 79.56% of the running words in the MS-CAT Corpus. In comparison, the GSL covered 76.1% of Coxhead's Academic Corpus, which is a difference of about 3.5% in coverage. (See Table B.3 for the comparisons of coverage between the two corpora.) This was evidence of the difference in vocabulary between a corpus of textbooks written for students in middle school and one of university-level texts: middle school textbooks contain more high-frequency vocabulary than do texts written for students at the university level. In addition, the AWL words cover 5.37% of the MS-CAT Corpus. Those same words represent 10% of Coxhead's Academic Corpus, so we can again see a difference in coverage between the two corpora.

Table B.3. Comparison of coverage of the Academic Corpus and the Middle School Content-Area Textbook Corpus by the General Service List (GSL) and the Academic Word List (AWL)

Word list	Corpora	
	Academic Corpus[a]	Middle School Content-Area Textbook Corpus
Number of General Service List (GSL)[b] families	1968	1979
Number of Academic Word List (AWL)[a] families	570	568
GSL text coverage (%)	76.1	79.56
AWL text coverage (%)	10.0	5.37
Total (%)	86.1	84.93

[a]Coxhead (2000).
[b]West (1953).

When taken together, the GSL and the AWL covered 84.93% of the MS-CAT Corpus, nearly the same coverage of the combined lists over Coxhead's Academic Corpus (86.1%). The reason for this balance was a higher percentage of GSL words combined with a lower percentage of AWL words in the MS-CAT Corpus.

It is interesting to note that all but two of the word families on the AWL were present in the MS-CAT Corpus (*intrinsic* and *paradigm* were the exceptions), but although the AWL word families were present, many family members simply did not appear with the same frequency as they did in Coxhead's Academic Corpus. This result was not surprising, given the difference in the purposes of these two corpora. The next challenge was to identify a different set of words, one that included all of the qualifying AWL words plus any additional words that met the same frequency criteria Coxhead initiated when she created the AWL. This process will be described in the next subsection.

Identification of Middle School Academic Vocabulary Words

Following Coxhead's methodology, GSL words were purposely excluded from the Middle School Vocabulary Lists. Beyond those words, the first group of words identified for the lists were AWL word family members that met the following criteria: 1) for range, a minimum frequency of 11.4 times per million words in each of the five content-area subcorpora, and 2) a minimum frequency of 28.5 times per million words within the MS-CAT Corpus. Proportionally, these are the same range and frequency cuts used by Coxhead (2000). AWL family members meeting these criteria are included in all five of the Middle School Vocabulary Lists.

The second group of words identified for the Middle School Vocabulary Lists are AWL family members occurring with minimum frequencies of 28.5 times per million words within the MS-CAT Corpus and 11.4 times per million words in a specific content-area subcorpora. This cut provided the opportunity to capture individual AWL words that occurred frequently within a single content area but not frequently in all content areas. AWL family members meeting these criteria were added to their related content-area word list.

A third cut was made, this time with the intent of identifying frequently occurring words that were not part of the AWL yet occurred with the same minimum range and frequency cuts that Coxhead used when developing the AWL (11.4 times per million words in each of the content-area subcorpora and 28.5 times per million words in the MS-CAT Corpus). Words meeting these criteria were added to each of the Middle School Vocabulary Lists.

Finally, the fourth cut included words that were not part of the AWL, but occurred with a minimum frequency of 100 times per million words in a specific subcorpus. These identified words were added to their related content-area word list and represent the frequently occurring technical vocabulary contained within each of the content-area subcorpora.

This procedure marks a departure from Coxhead's AWL development. Coxhead built her lists using a top-down process. First she identified frequently occurring types and built up the word families around them. Once all family members were in place, she was able to see how well the AWL word families covered the Academic Corpus.

The Middle School Vocabulary List families were built using a bottom-up process. With the exception of missing headwords, the family members on the Middle School Vocabulary Lists are those that met criteria for range and frequency either in the MS-CAT Corpus or in its content-area subcorpora.

Organization of the Middle School Vocabulary Lists

There are five different content-area vocabulary lists, one for each of the subject areas of English grammar and writing, health, mathematics, science, and social studies and history. Once qualifying words were identified for a specific list, those words were organized into word families, and if the headword for that family was not present in terms of frequency, it was added to the list (e.g., the headword *depress* was added to the family members *depression* and *depressed*). From a pedagogical standpoint, it would not make sense to have family members present without their related headword. Other than headwords, no additional family members were included. Limiting family members to those that qualified in terms of range and frequency was a purposeful decision that allows word list users to focus on the inflected and affixed forms that occur most frequently in textbooks written for middle school students. Proper nouns, acronyms, and abbreviations are not present on these lists, which is consistent with the methodology used in the creation of frequency-based word lists. Table B.4 provides the numbers of word types and word families in each of the Middle School Vocabulary Lists.

RESULTS

Range analysis shows that when combined with the words on the GSL, the Middle School Vocabulary Lists provide coverage for their corresponding subcorpora that is consistent with the coverage provided by the AWL over the Academic Corpus. Chapter 2 in this book provides a complete discussion of the text coverage of these lists, and Table 2.1 illustrates the text coverage of each of the Middle School Vocabulary Lists.

VALIDATION OF THE MIDDLE SCHOOL CONTENT-AREA VOCABULARY LISTS

A frequency-based word list should be expected to cover the corpus from which it was developed, but to determine whether it really is a good list it must be checked against a second corpus. Following Coxhead's (2000) methodology, a parallel corpus was created containing a separate set of content-area textbooks written for middle school students in each of the five content areas (see Table B.5 for the running word composition of the parallel corpus). Just as in the development of the MS-CAT Corpus, the parallel corpus was broken into subcorpora for each grade level and content area. If the words on the Middle School Vocabulary Lists represented similarly high coverage of the parallel corpus and its subcorpora, they could be considered valid lists. As detailed in Table B.6, Range analysis results demonstrated similarly strong coverage of the subcorpora of the parallel corpus by their corresponding word lists.

Table B.4. Word types and word families in the Middle School Vocabulary Lists

Middle School Vocabulary List	Number of word types	Number of word families
English grammar and writing	722	374
Heath	802	406
Mathematics	616	321
Science	859	435
Social studies and history	809	394

Table B.5. Running word composition of the subcorpora of the parallel corpus

	Subcorpora of the parallel corpus					
	English grammar and writing	Health	Mathematics	Science	Social studies and history	Total
Number of running words	390,080	566,654	1,643,061	1,608,059	1,689,157	8,897,011

There was one final test to be sure that the words on the Middle School Vocabulary Lists were truly academic in nature. Again, following Coxhead's (2000) methodology, the lists were tested against a corpus of middle school reading and literature textbooks containing 5,678,676 running words. Because these textbooks contain a great deal of fiction, they are considered a different genre from academic texts. The expectation was that there would be a higher presence of GSL words and a lower presence of academic words in this corpus than in a corpus of strictly academic texts. As shown in Table B.7, Range analysis showed the GSL covered 83.75% of the literature corpus, which was a higher percentage than in any of the content-area subcorpora. The Middle School Vocabulary Lists' coverage of the subcorpora ranged from 1.73% (mathematics) to 2.89% (English grammar and writing). In Coxhead's study, the AWL covered 1.4% of a fictional corpus, so whereas these percentages are higher, it is important to note that there is instructional text embedded in reading and literature textbooks, and for this reason, it was expected that there would be a greater presence of academic vocabulary in this corpus than in Coxhead's corpus of fictional texts.

Table B.6. Coverage of the parallel subcorpora by the General Service List and the Middle School Vocabulary Lists

	Subcorpora of the parallel corpus				
Word list coverage	English grammar and writing	Health	Mathematics	Science	Social studies and history
General Service List[a] (%)	82.41	84.00	79.45	79.36	78.53
Middle School Vocabulary List (%)	6.08	8.17	9.41	9.48	5.95
Total (%)	88.49	92.17	88.86	88.84	84.48

[a]West (1953).

Table B.7. Coverage of the literature subcorpus by the General Service List and the Middle School Vocabulary Lists

	Middle School Vocabulary List				
Word list coverage	English grammar and writing	Health	Mathematics	Science	Social studies and history
General Service List[a] (%)	83.75	83.75	83.75	83.75	83.75
Middle School Vocabulary List (%)	2.89	2.11	1.73	2.09	2.48
Total (%)	88.64	85.86	85.48	85.84	86.23

[a]West (1953).

Based upon the results of these two tests, we can conclude that the Middle School Vocabulary Lists are a good representation of the academic vocabulary contained in content-area textbooks written for middle school students. Knowing these words in addition to the words on the GSL provides students the ability to understand a large percentage of the words they encounter in their course textbooks. In the next section, we describe the limitations of the Middle School Vocabulary Lists and address some of the potential criticisms associated with their development.

LIMITATIONS AND POTENTIAL CRITICISMS OF THE MIDDLE SCHOOL VOCABULARY LISTS

Any word list that is built from another takes on the limitations of the earlier list (Coxhead, 2000). The Middle School Vocabulary Lists were built on top of the GSL, which is an old list and is in need of revision; however, at the time the Middle School Vocabulary Lists were created, no updated versions were available. Recently, Brezina and Gablasova (2013) published a new list of general service vocabulary. Current research on this list is underway to determine if it does a better job than the GSL. Although that question is presently unresolved, we still know that the GSL demonstrates excellent coverage of the MS-CAT Corpus and the content-area subcorpora.

In addition to being built on top of the GSL, the methodology used for creating the Middle School Vocabulary Lists included a purposeful selection of AWL family members. For this reason, the criticisms directed at the AWL regarding the need for discipline-specific word identification (Davies & Gardner, 2013; Hyland & Tse, 2007; Martinez et al., 2009) might also be directed toward these lists. However, the methodology used to compile the Middle School Vocabulary Lists was specific in including AWL words that frequently appear within specific subcorpora in addition to those that occurred frequently in the MS-CAT Corpus as a whole. In addition, words that were not part of the AWL were included as well. Words were included that met the same range and frequency criteria, both across the MS-CAT Corpus and within specific subcorpora, which helps to make the Middle School Vocabulary Lists more discipline-specific and should help to circumvent this problem.

A second area of criticism is that, like the AWL, the words contained on the Middle School Vocabulary Lists are not presented in authentic contexts. In response to this concern, more research on academic words in context is always useful, because it can provide valuable information about usage patterns, collocations, grammatical patterns, variations in use, and so on. However, such detail is beyond the scope of this study, which was to identify the most frequently occurring academic words contained in a corpus of written texts used by middle school students. Discipline-specific word lists containing the most frequently occurring multiword units would be useful for teachers and learners, but such work has yet to appear.

A third area of concern is that frequency-based word list creation does not allow for human judgment in determining a word's relative importance, and some words that really are important may be omitted from a list because they did not make the frequency cut (Marzano, 2004). Toward this point, the Middle School Vocabulary Lists contain many technical terms (e.g., *cell, energy, atom*) for each content area, but they do not contain all, or even most, of them.

Earlier in this book, we discussed the tensions involved in creating word lists. Frequency-based word list creators want to identify the fewest number of words that provide the greatest amount of text coverage. The technical terms identified for these lists had to occur with a minimum frequency of 100 times per million words within their content-area subcorpus. The difficulty is that when researchers widen the net, so to speak, to identify more words, those identified words provide incrementally smaller amounts of text coverage. So, using the science subcorpus as an example, had the cut for technical words been increased to a minimum frequency of 50 times per million words, an additional 216 families (274 words) would have been identified, resulting in a list of 651 families (currently there are 435 families on the Middle School Science Academic Vocabulary List), but those additional 216 families would have only increased the text coverage by 1.82%. The result would have been a much longer list of words, making it more difficult for teachers and word learners to use.

Researchers have provided many different lists of words, created using just as many methodologies, and each of these lists carries its own set of limitations related to its methodology. For this reason, teachers and students should not limit their word-study choices to the words on any given list. The purpose of a frequency-based word list is to focus attention on words that students will encounter most frequently, which maximizes the benefit of the time invested in word learning.

SUMMARY

We began this appendix with principles and issues surrounding corpus design, and described the development of a corpus of middle school texts and the creation of word lists derived from this corpus, as well as their possible limitations. We have found that although none of these lists provides students with the 95%–98% text coverage needed for instructional and independent reading, the Middle School Vocabulary Lists, taken with the words on the GSL and proper nouns, consistently provide coverage around the 90% mark, which makes these lists truly useful for middle grades students, their teachers, and materials writers.

Appendix

Vocabulary Size Test Version A

The following is a version of the Vocabulary Size Test. This version is also available online at http://www.victoria.ac.nz/lals/about/staff/publications/paul-nation/VST-version-A.pdf.

1. **see** They *saw it*.
    a closed it tightly
    b waited for it
    c looked at it
    d started it up

2. **time** They have a lot of *time*.
    a money
    b food
    c hours
    d friends

3. **period** It was a difficult *period*.
    a question
    b time
    c thing to do
    d book

4. **figure** Is this the right *figure*?
    a answer
    b place
    c time
    d number

5. **poor** We *are poor*.
    a have no money
    b feel happy
    c are very interested
    d do not like to work hard

6. **microphone** Please use the *microphone*.
    a machine for making food hot
    b machine that makes sounds louder
    c machine that makes things look bigger
    d small telephone that can be carried around

From Nation, I.S.P. (n.d.). *Vocabulary size test version A*. Retrieved from http://www.victoria.ac.nz/lals/about/staff/publications/paul-nation/VST-version-A.pdf; reprinted by permission. In *Academic Vocabulary for Middle School Students: Research-Based Lists and Strategies for Key Content Areas* by Jennifer Wells Greene & Averil Coxhead (2015; Paul H. Brookes Publishing Co.).

7. **nil**   His mark for that question was *nil*.
   a   very bad
   b   nothing
   c   very good
   d   in the middle

8. **pub**   They went to the *pub*.
   a   place where people drink and talk
   b   place that looks after money
   c   large building with many shops
   d   building for swimming

9. **circle**   Make a *circle*.
   a   rough picture
   b   space with nothing in it
   c   round shape
   d   large hole

10. **dig**   Our dog often *digs*.
   a   solves problems with things
   b   creates a hole in the ground
   c   wants to sleep
   d   enters the water

11. **soldier**   He is a *soldier*.
   a   person in a business
   b   person who studies
   c   person who uses metal
   d   person in the army

12. **restore**   It has been *restored*.
   a   said again
   b   given to a different person
   c   made like new again
   d   given a lower price

13. **pro**   He's *a pro*.
   a   someone who is employed to find out important secrets
   b   a stupid person
   c   someone who writes for a newspaper
   d   someone who is paid for playing sport

14. **compound**   They made a new *compound*.
   a   agreement
   b   thing made of two or more parts
   c   group of people forming a business
   d   guess based on past experience

15. **deficit**   The company *had a large deficit*.
   a   spent a lot more money than it earned
   b   went down a lot in value
   c   had a plan for its spending that used a lot of money
   d   had a lot of money stored in the bank

16. **strap**   He broke the *strap*.
   a   promise
   b   top cover
   c   shallow dish for food
   d   strip of strong material

17. **weep**   He *wept*.
   a   finished his course
   b   cried
   c   died
   d   worried

18. **haunt**   The house is *haunted*.
   a   full of decorations
   b   rented
   c   empty
   d   full of ghosts

19. **cube**   I need one more *cube*.
   a   sharp thing used for joining things
   b   solid square block
   c   tall cup with no saucer
   d   piece of stiff paper folded in half

20. **butler**   They have a *butler*.
   a   man servant
   b   machine for cutting up trees
   c   private teacher
   d   cool dark room under the house

From Nation, I.S.P. (n.d.). *Vocabulary size test version A*. Retrieved from http://www.victoria.ac.nz/lals/about/staff/publications/paul-nation/VST-version-A.pdf; reprinted by permission. In *Academic Vocabulary for Middle School Students: Research-Based Lists and Strategies for Key Content Areas* by Jennifer Wells Greene & Averil Coxhead (2015; Paul H. Brookes Publishing Co.).

21. **nun**   We saw a *nun*.
    a long thin creature that lives in the earth
    b terrible accident
    c woman following a strict religious life
    d unexplained bright light in the sky

22. **olive**   We bought *olives*.
    a oily fruit
    b scented flowers
    c men's swimming clothes
    d tools for digging

23. **shudder**   The boy *shuddered*.
    a spoke with a low voice
    b almost fell
    c shook
    d called out loudly

24. **threshold**   They raised the *threshold*.
    a flag
    b point or line where something changes
    c roof inside a building
    d cost of borrowing money

25. **demography**   This book is about *demography*.
    a the study of patterns of land use
    b the study of the use of pictures to show facts about numbers
    c the study of the movement of water
    d the study of population

26. **malign**   His *malign* influence is still felt.
    a good
    b evil
    c very important
    d secret

27. **strangle**   He *strangled* her.
    a killed her by pressing her throat
    b gave her all the things she wanted
    c took her away by force
    d admired her greatly

28. **dinosaur**   The children were pretending to be *dinosaurs*.
    a robbers who work at sea
    b very small creatures with human form but with wings
    c large creatures with wings that breathe fire
    d animals that lived an extremely long time ago

29. **jug**   He was holding *a jug*.
    a a container for pouring liquids
    b an informal discussion
    c a soft cap
    d a weapon that blows up

30. **crab**   Do you like *crabs*?
    a very thin small cakes
    b tight, hard collars
    c sea creatures that always walk to one side
    d large black insects that sing at night

31. **quilt**   They made a *quilt*.
    a statement about who should get their property when they die
    b firm agreement
    c thick warm cover for a bed
    d feather pen

32. **tummy**   Look at my *tummy*.
    a fabric to cover the head
    b stomach
    c small soft animal
    d finger used for gripping

33. **eclipse**   *There was an eclipse*.
    a A strong wind blew all day
    b I heard something hit the water
    c A large number of people were killed
    d The sun was hidden by the moon

34. **excrete**   This was *excreted* recently.
    a pushed or sent out
    b made clear
    c discovered by a science experiment
    d put on a list of illegal things

From Nation, I.S.P. (n.d.). *Vocabulary size test version A*. Retrieved from http://www.victoria.ac.nz/lals/about/staff/publications/paul-nation/VST-version-A.pdf; reprinted by permission. In *Academic Vocabulary for Middle School Students: Research-Based Lists and Strategies for Key Content Areas* by Jennifer Wells Greene & Averil Coxhead (2015; Paul H. Brookes Publishing Co.).

35. **ubiquitous**   Many unwanted plants *are ubiquitous.*
    a   are difficult to get rid of
    b   have long, strong roots
    c   are found everywhere
    d   die away in the winter

36. **marrow**   This is *the marrow.*
    a   symbol that brings good luck to a team
    b   soft center of a bone
    c   control for guiding a plane
    d   increase in salary

37. **cabaret**   We saw the *cabaret.*
    a   painting covering a whole wall
    b   song and dance performance
    c   small crawling creature
    d   person who is half fish, half woman

38. **cavalier**   He treated her *in a cavalier manner.*
    a   without care
    b   with good manners
    c   awkwardly
    d   as a brother would

39. **veer**   The car *veered.*
    a   moved shakily
    b   changed course
    c   made a very loud noise
    d   slid without the wheels turning

40. **yogurt**   This *yogurt* is disgusting.
    a   dark gray mud found at the bottom of rivers
    b   unhealthy, open sore
    c   thick, soured milk, often with sugar and flavoring
    d   large purple fruit with soft flesh

41. **octopus**   They saw *an octopus.*
    a   a large bird that hunts at night
    b   a ship that can go under water
    c   a machine that flies by means of turning blades
    d   a sea creature with eight legs

42. **monologue**   Now he has a *monologue.*
    a   single piece of glass to hold over his eye to help him to see
    b   long turn at talking without being interrupted
    c   position with all the power
    d   picture made by joining letters together in interesting ways

43. **candid**   Please *be candid.*
    a   be careful
    b   show sympathy
    c   show fairness to both sides
    d   say what you really think

44. **nozzle**   Aim the *nozzle* toward it.
    a   space that light passes through in a camera
    b   dry patch of skin
    c   pipe attachment that forces water
    d   sharp part of a fork

45. **psychosis**   He has *a psychosis.*
    a   an inability to move
    b   an oddly colored patch of skin
    c   a body organ that processes sugar
    d   a mental illness

46. **ruckus**   He got hurt in the *ruckus.*
    a   region between the stomach and the top of the leg
    b   noisy street fight
    c   group of players gathered round the ball in some ball games
    d   race across a field of snow

47. **ruble**   He had a lot of *rubles.*
    a   very valuable red stones
    b   distant members of his family
    c   Russian money
    d   moral or other difficulties in the mind

From Nation, I.S.P. (n.d.). *Vocabulary size test version A.* Retrieved from http://www.victoria.ac.nz/lals/about/staff/publications/paul-nation/VST-version-A.pdf; reprinted by permission. In *Academic Vocabulary for Middle School Students: Research-Based Lists and Strategies for Key Content Areas* by Jennifer Wells Greene & Averil Coxhead (2015; Paul H. Brookes Publishing Co.).

48. **canonical** These are *canonical examples.*
    a examples that break the usual rules
    b examples taken from a religious book
    c regular and widely accepted examples
    d examples discovered very recently

49. **puree** This *puree* is bright green.
    a fruit or vegetables in liquid form
    b dress worn by women in India
    c skin of a fruit
    d very thin material for evening dresses

50. **vial** Put it in a *vial.*
    a device that stores electricity
    b country residence
    c dramatic scene
    d small glass bottle

51. **counterclaim** They made *a counterclaim.*
    a a demand response made by one side in a law case
    b a request for a shop to take back things with faults
    c an agreement between two companies to exchange work
    d a decorative cover for a bed, which is always on top

52. **refectory** We met in the *refectory.*
    a room for eating
    b office where legal papers can be signed
    c room for several people to sleep in
    d room with glass walls for growing plants

53. **trill** He practiced the *trill.*
    a repeated high musical sound
    b type of stringed instrument
    c way of throwing the ball
    d dance step of turning round very fast on the toes

54. **talon** Just look at those *talons*!
    a high points of mountains
    b sharp hooks on the feet of a hunting bird
    c heavy metal coats to protect against weapons
    d people who make fools of themselves without realizing it

55. **plankton** We saw a lot of *plankton* here.
    a poisonous plants that spread very quickly
    b very small plants or animals found in water
    c trees producing hard wood
    d gray soil that often causes land to slip

56. **soliloquy** That was an excellent *soliloquy*!
    a song for six people
    b short clever saying with a deep meaning
    c entertainment using lights and music
    d speech in the theatre by a character who is alone

57. **puma** They saw a *puma.*
    a small house made of mud bricks
    b tree from hot, dry countries
    c large wild cat
    d very strong wind that lifts anything in its path

58. **augur** It *augured well.*
    a promised good things for the future
    b agreed with what was expected
    c had a color that looked good with something else
    d rang with a clear, beautiful sound

59. **emir**   We saw the *emir*.
    a   bird with two long curved tail feathers
    b   woman who cares for other people's children in eastern countries
    c   Middle Eastern chief with power in his own land
    d   house made from blocks of ice

60. **didactic**   The story *is very didactic*.
    a   tries hard to teach something
    b   is very difficult to believe
    c   deals with exciting actions
    d   is written with unclear meaning

61. **cranny**   Look what we found in the *cranny*!
    a   sale of unwanted objects
    b   narrow opening
    c   space for storing things under the roof of a house
    d   large wooden box

62. **lectern**   He stood at the *lectern*.
    a   desk made to hold a book at a good height for reading
    b   table or block used for church ceremonies
    c   place where you buy drinks
    d   very edge

63. **azalea**   This *azalea* is very pretty.
    a   small tree with many flowers growing in groups
    b   light natural fabric
    c   long piece of material worn in India
    d   seashell shaped like a fan

64. **marsupial**   It is *a marsupial*.
    a   an animal with hard feet
    b   a plant that takes several years to grow
    c   a plant with flowers that turn to face the sun
    d   an animal with a pocket for babies

65. **bawdy**   It was very *bawdy*.
    a   unpredictable
    b   innocent
    c   rushed
    d   indecent

66. **crowbar**   He used a *crowbar*.
    a   heavy iron pole with a curved end
    b   false name
    c   sharp tool for making holes in leather
    d   light metal walking stick

67. **spangled**   Her dress was *spangled*.
    a   torn into thin strips
    b   covered with small bright decorations
    c   made with lots of folds of fabric
    d   ruined by touching something very hot

68. **aver**   She *averred* that it was the truth.
    a   refused to agree
    b   declared
    c   believed
    d   warned

69. **retro**   It had *a retro look*.
    a   a very fashionable look
    b   the look of a piece of modern art
    c   the look of something that has been used a lot before
    d   the look of something from an earlier time

70. **rascal**   She is such *a rascal* sometimes.
    a   an unbeliever
    b   a dedicated student
    c   a hard worker
    d   a bad girl

71. **tweezers**   They used *tweezers*.
    a   small pieces of metal for holding papers together
    b   small pieces of string for closing wounds
    c   a tool with two blades for picking up or holding small objects
    d   strong tool for cutting plants

From Nation, I.S.P. (n.d.). *Vocabulary size test version A*. Retrieved from http://www.victoria.ac.nz/lals/about/staff/publications/paul-nation/VST-version-A.pdf; reprinted by permission. In *Academic Vocabulary for Middle School Students: Research-Based Lists and Strategies for Key Content Areas* by Jennifer Wells Greene & Averil Coxhead (2015; Paul H. Brookes Publishing Co.).

72. **bidet**   They have a *bidet.*
   a low basin for washing the body after using the toilet
   b large fierce brown dog
   c small private swimming pool
   d man to help in the house

73. **sloop**   Whose *sloop* is that?
   a warm hat
   b light sailing boat
   c left over food
   d untidy work

74. **swingeing**   They got *swingeing fines.*
   a very large fines
   b very small fines
   c fines paid in small amounts at a time
   d fines that vary depending on income

75. **cenotaph**   We met at the *cenotaph.*
   a large and important church
   b public square in the center of a town
   c memorial for people buried somewhere else
   d underground train station

76. **denouement**   I was disappointed with the *denouement.*
   a ending of a story that solves the mystery
   b amount of money paid for a piece of work
   c small place to live that is part of a bigger building
   d official report of the results of a political meeting

77. **bittern**   She saw a *bittern.*
   a large bottle for storing liquid
   b small green grass snake
   c false picture caused by hot air
   d water bird with long legs and a very loud call

78. **reconnoiter**   They have gone to *reconnoiter.*
   a think again
   b make an examination of a new place
   c have a good time to mark a happy event
   d complain formally

79. **magnanimity**   We will never forget her *magnanimity.*
   a very offensive and unfriendly manners
   b courage in times of trouble
   c generosity
   d completely sincere words

80. **effete**   He has become *effete.*
   a weak and soft
   b too fond of strong drink
   c unable to leave his bed
   d extremely easy to annoy

81. **rollick**   They were *rollicking.*
   a driving very fast
   b staying away from school without being permitted to
   c having fun in a noisy and spirited way
   d sliding on snow using round boards

82. **gobbet**   The cat left a *gobbet* behind.
   a strip of torn material
   b footprint
   c piece of solid waste from the body
   d lump of food returned from the stomach

83. **rigmarole**   I hate the *rigmarole.*
   a very fast and difficult dance for eight people
   b funny character in the theatre
   c form that must be completed each year for tax purposes
   d long, pointless, and complicated set of actions

84. **alimony**   The article was about *alimony*.
    a feelings of bitterness and annoyance, expressed sharply
    b money for the care of children, paid regularly after a divorce
    c giving praise for excellent ideas
    d a metal that breaks easily and is bluish white

85. **roughshod**   He *rode roughshod*.
    a traveled without good preparation
    b made lots of mistakes
    c did not consider other people's feelings
    d did not care about his own comfort

86. **copra**   They supply *copra*.
    a a highly poisonous substance used to kill unwanted plants
    b the dried meat from a large nut used to make oil
    c an illegal substance that makes people feel good for a short time
    d strong rope used on sailing ships

87. **bier**   She lay on the *bier*.
    a folding garden chair
    b grass next to a river
    c place where boats can be tied up
    d board on which a dead body is carried

88. **torpid**   He was *in a torpid state*.
    a undecided
    b filled with very strong feelings
    c confused and anxious
    d slow and sleepy

89. **dachshund**   She loves her *dachshund*.
    a warm fur hat
    b thick floor rug with special patterns
    c small dog with short legs and a long back
    d old musical instrument with twelve strings

90. **cadenza**   What did you think of the *cadenza*?
    a cake topped with cream and fruit
    b large box hanging from a wire that carries people up a mountain
    c slow formal dance from Italy
    d passage in a piece of music that shows the player's great skill

91. **obtrude**   These thoughts *obtruded themselves*.
    a got themselves lost or forgotten
    b did not agree with each other
    c got mixed up with each other
    d pushed themselves forward in the mind

92. **panzer**   They saw the *panzers* getting nearer.
    a players in a marching band
    b fighter planes
    c large, slow windowless army cars
    d policewomen

93. **cyborg**   She read about *a cyborg*.
    a an integrated human-machine system
    b a musical instrument with forty strings
    c a small, newly invented object
    d a warm wind in winter

94. **zygote**   It is *a zygote*.
    a an early phase of sexual reproduction
    b a lot of bother over nothing
    c a small animal found in southern Africa
    d a gun used to launch rockets

95. **sylvan**   The painting had a *sylvan* theme.
    a lost love
    b wandering
    c forest
    d casual folk

96. **sagacious** She had many ideas that were *sagacious.*
    a instinctively clever
    b ridiculous and wild
    c about abusing people and being abused
    d rebellious and dividing

97. **spatiotemporal** My theory is *spatiotemporal.*
    a focused on small details
    b annoying to people
    c objectionably modern
    d oriented to time and space

98. **casuist** Don't *play the casuist* with me!
    a focus only on self-pleasure
    b act like a tough guy
    c make judgments about my conduct of duty
    d be stupid

99. **cyberpunk** I like *cyberpunk.*
    a medicine that does not use drugs
    b one variety of science fiction
    c the art and science of eating
    d a society ruled by technical experts

100. **pussyfoot** Let's not *pussyfoot around.*
    a criticize unreasonably
    b take care to avoid confrontation
    c attack indirectly
    d suddenly start

From Nation, I.S.P. (n.d.). *Vocabulary size test version A.* Retrieved from http://www.victoria.ac.nz/lals/about/staff/publications/paul-nation/VST-version-A.pdf; reprinted by permission. In *Academic Vocabulary for Middle School Students: Research-Based Lists and Strategies for Key Content Areas* by Jennifer Wells Greene & Averil Coxhead (2015; Paul H. Brookes Publishing Co.).

VOCABULARY SIZE TEST ANSWERS

The following is the answer key of the version of the Vocabulary Size Test above. This answer key is also available online at http://www.victoria.ac.nz/lals/about/staff/publications/paul-nation/VST-version-A_answers.pdf.

1. see	c	
2. time	c	
3. period	b	
4. figure	d	
5. poor	a	
6. microphone	b	
7. nil	b	
8. pub	a	
9. circle	c	
10. dig	b	
11. soldier	d	
12. restore	c	
13. pro	d	
14. compound	b	
15. deficit	a	
16. strap	d	
17. weep	b	
18. haunt	d	
19. cube	b	
20. butler	a	
21. nun	c	
22. olive	a	
23. shudder	c	
24. threshold	b	
25. demography	d	
26. malign	b	
27. strangle	a	
28. dinosaur	d	
29. jug	a	
30. crab	c	
31. quilt	c	
32. tummy	b	
33. eclipse	d	
34. excrete	a	

35. ubiquitous	c	
36. marrow	b	
37. cabaret	b	
38. cavalier	a	
39. veer	b	
40. yogurt	c	
41. octopus	d	
42. monologue	b	
43. candid	d	
44. nozzle	c	
45. psychosis	d	
46. ruckus	c	
47. ruble	c	
48. canonical	c	
49. puree	a	
50. vial	d	
51. counterclaim	a	
52. refectory	a	
53. trill	a	
54. talon	b	
55. plankton	b	
56. soliloquy	d	
57. puma	c	
58. augur	a	
59. emir	c	
60. didactic	a	
61. cranny	b	
62. lectern	a	
63. azalea	a	
64. marsupial	d	
65. bawdy	d	
66. crowbar	a	
67. spangled	b	
68. aver	b	

69. retro	d	
70. rascal	d	
71. tweezers	c	
72. bidet	a	
73. sloop	b	
74. swingeing	a	
75. cenotaph	c	
76. denouement	a	
77. bittern	d	
78. reconnoiter	b	
79. magnanimity	c	
80. effete	a	
81. rollick	c	
82. gobbet	d	
83. rigmarole	d	
84. alimony	b	
85. roughshod	c	
86. copra	b	
87. bier	d	
88. torpid	d	
89. dachshund	c	
90. cadenza	d	
91. obtrude	d	
92. panzer	c	
93. cyborg	a	
94. zygote	a	
95. sylvan	c	
96. sagacious	a	
97. spatiotemporal	d	
98. casuist	c	
99. cyberpunk	b	
100. pussyfoot	b	

Index

Page numbers followed by *f* and *t* indicate figures and tables, respectively.